D1562672

AN INSIDER'S VIEW OF A
Principal's Life:
Eyewitness Narratives
from the Neighborhood

Dr. Alice Siegel, Dr. Yolanda Ramirez,
Dr. Marlene Zakierski

Print ISBN: 978-1-09831-191-9

eBook ISBN: 978-1-09831-192-6

We dedicate this book to:

All those school leaders who work daily to make a positive
impact on children and their communities

CONTENTS

INTRODUCTION

The role of the principalship is one of the most arduous, yet one of the most rewarding, positions within a school setting. As school leaders become more grounded in the complexity of the work, they begin to learn how to navigate a multitude of situations. According to Bennis (2009), "creative problem solving is a form of innovative learning" and in "innovative learning, one must not only recognize existing contexts, but be capable of imagining future contexts" (p 71).

This book shows our appreciation for the incredible work school leaders perform on a daily basis and it informs all parents who have or had children enrolled in school—public, charter or private—of the many facets that are integral to school leaders responsibilities. Additionally, it is hoped that the book will be of interest and applicable to all educators: teachers, administrators, teacher assistants, and other school personnel, as these stories can and have occurred in various PreK–12 schools in different parts of the United States. Also it is hoped that district leaders, parents, and other school personnel will gain insight into important issues, concerns, and sometimes humorous situations administrators deal with on a daily basis.

The book may also be used as a text in educational leadership classes on both the masters and doctoral levels or in a professional development setting for newly appointed principals.

It is always helpful for those entering the field of education to know that they are not alone in handling similar situations. In the classroom setting, professors can use the text to promote discussion among small groups of future administrators. The scenarios can also serve as case studies that will ignite meaningful class discussions and ideas surrounding real issues that can offer alternative interpretations of the many challenges faced by educational administrators in the world of leadership. To that end, suggested discussion questions are presented to spark conversations regarding possible solutions as an addendum. Please note that all stories in the book are real and were told to the authors by public, charter and or private school principals from different parts of the United States. All names, locales and dates have been changed to protect both the principal and the people involved in the stories.

All three authors have doctoral degrees in educational and instructional leadership. Collectively, they have a combined total of more than 100 years in the field of education, with more than forty years as appointed principals. Two of the authors are currently professors in a doctoral program. All have worked in diverse as well as gentrified school communities, creating successful learning environments for all children. Given current events in the field of education, they understand how important it is to share their experiences with both new and senior school leaders. These stories span from humorous and outrageous to the difficult situations that principals must learn to navigate on a daily basis. All are actual stories recounted by a diverse group of school leaders. The authors hope that these stories may be used to help present and future administrators as they grapple with making leadership decisions. When school leaders decide on a solution, they must also think about how that solution will affect forthcoming decisions and possibly school policy.

First and foremost, the principal has an enormous responsibility to ensure that children are achieving individual academic success. And of course, teachers must be observed, provided feedback, and evaluated to determine the next steps in their professional development. As school leaders, principals try to immerse themselves in the surrounding community. They build relationships with community-based organizations and local politicians, and generally are the first stop for parents who have questions and concerns about almost anything. To the outsider, it may be difficult to understand how many situations actually sit on the desk of the principal. In fact, it is not the spats from children that become the more difficult part of leadership. Bolman and Deal (2008) asserted that leadership is different as compared to other types of relationships because leadership allows individuals to join forces together with shared visions, values, and missions (p 3). In order to build those collegial connections or liaisons, a large part of the principals' work requires skillful listening, negotiations, and final decision making from parent complaints, interesting requests, and overall concerns.

Parents may have the best intentions in mind for their child, but they are not knowledgeable of the whole school situation. As a result, this presents a slippery slope for decision making by the principal. In Bolman and Deal's(2006), The Wizard and Warrior, the authors select various leaders to exemplify the roles and paths of warriors and wizards to achieve successful results. Bolman and Deal (2006) posit "Though the potentials for wizard and warrior coexist in all of us, our gifts differ, and some of us are more determined than others to develop and use the gifts we have" (p 162). Furthermore they state, "The wizard relies more heavily on magic and mystery, the warrior on strength and skill" (p 163). As a principal, one's aspect of the various situations encountered call for either wizard or warrior skills to achieve successful results.

This book intends to share some of the requests that a principal is challenged to negotiate daily. Although the examples range from serious to outlandish, these are daily issues that principals must unpack and respond to successfully within their school communities. With all of these issues in the laps of principals, it is a wonder how they maintain their sanity and continue to lead successful schools.

SECTION ONE:

The Ever-Exciting Lunchroom

One of the most fascinating and energetic parts of the school day is the lunch period. It is a place where children are free to have conversations that are simply out of this world with their pals! It is one of the most notable parts of the school day, serving as a place where children can talk about anything. The lunchroom does not mimic the monotonous tone of the local diner. It is, in fact, as loud as fireworks being set off in the living room on the Fourth of July. The lunchroom is an important part of a child's education, a splendid place for socialization, friendly debate, lots of fun and a time to share interests of all kinds. It is simply a time of day that exudes a pure burst of kid energy.

Schools can have upward of four lunch periods a day, depending on how many children are registered in the school. These lunch periods can begin as early as ten forty-five in the morning. Scheduling also presents a few challenges at times, dependent upon student and staff attendance. These issues affect the lunch schedules and present a challenge to support a smooth and safe lunch period.

As the winter months approach, lunchroom staff work together to make sure the lunchroom remains safe but also fun for the children. This becomes a difficult task, especially during inclement weather. At these times, school aides work with a supervisor to organize games and other activities, creating a fun atmosphere for eating and socializing. There can be as many as 200 children in a lunch period, with very limited staff or volunteers. The staff may schedule all of the children to eat together and then go out to recess. Other times, they may have split lunches, where half of the children go to recess while the rest eat inside. They trade places after twenty to twenty-five minutes in each area. Many parents worry that the swapped lunch period shortens the time children have to sit, eat, and spend time with their friends. Yet, this procedure works well in many school locations with adequate staffing.

Watching movies and playing games are other activities that take place at lunchtime. Movies are tricky, since some parents prefer their child read or engage in a physical activity instead. Many children bring their books for independent reading. However, it is difficult to offer physical activities for large numbers of children when temperatures fall below freezing for multiple days. In an effort to offer children an activity when it becomes impossible to go outside, schools show pre-screened movies in the auditorium. Regardless of pre-screening, many parents will take issue with movie watching of any kind in a school, even during inclement weather. For this reason, schools also offer children board games, technology, and other activities of personal interest as they await the arrival of milder spring temperatures.

Given that there are many things to consider during lunch periods, there are many more challenges that the principal must face and consider to keep students and staff healthy and safe. The stories in this section are some of the many scenarios that happen during lunchtime in schools.

WHISTLE BLOWING

A parent came to see the principal about her displeasure with the lunchroom supervisor. She said that the lunchroom supervisor used a whistle in the lunchroom to quiet the children. She clearly told the principal "blowing a whistle is no way to handle children—that is the way you train animals." She demanded that the lunchroom supervisor go over to each child who needed to quiet down and behave. The principal disagreed and explained that the whistle was a signal to call or to get the children's attention, and this was the best way to communicate with a large group of children. Firmly, the principal explained that the aide could not and should not be running from child to child telling them to quiet down, and the whistle blowing continued.

ICE CREAM ANYONE?

A large group of elementary school parents met with the principal to express their concerns regarding items in the school vending machine. They also discussed the fact that ice cream was available for children to purchase following lunch periods and or after dismissal. One parent shared, "Children having access to the vending machines is a problem with obesity. When they come to school, snacks should not be made available for purchase." Another parent stated, "I like the idea of my child being able to buy something from the machine. I give them a dollar and they get to choose something they want either during the day or after school. I think this should be a parent's choice. If you don't want your child to have the snacks, then don't send them with money." Another parent said, "When it's hot outside, my kids love to have an ice cream cone. I don't mind my children having it and it's not like they eat it every day." Parents continued to speak to one another about the pros and cons of snack selection for children in elementary school, many demanding healthier choices and others wanting a combination of both. The principal thanked the parents for sharing their thoughts and with the promise of a follow-up, the meeting was concluded.

The next day, the principal met with her cabinet to discuss the parents concerns. They noticed that many children generally brought their snacks from home. It was agreed that if children wanted to use the vending machine or buy ice cream, it would be up to parents to decide on those treats. The school administration would meet with the vendor to discuss healthier snack options for the children. As the year progressed, the vending machine was stocked with many choices of healthy snack items for children. The cabinet members agreed that ice cream would remain for the rest of the year. However, in an effort to promote healthy snack, ice cream was eliminated as a daily snack choice in the school.

THE SEXY LUNCHROOM AIDE

Parents reported to the principal of an elementary school that the lunchroom aide, a very sexy-looking woman, was coming to work in inappropriate clothing and that the principal needed to investigate this situation. The lunchroom aide was a parent in the school, which required extra tact. When the principal observed the aide, she was leaning over a lunch room table wearing a very tight blouse and very short high cut, tight shorts. After her shift was over the principal went to see her and explained that the fifth and sixth grade boys found her too distracting. Upon hearing this, she became angry and walked away in a huff, yelling that she was quitting. The principal was surprised at her response and later found out that she told the parents the principal was jealous that she was young and sexy. The principal did not tell the parents of the actual interaction, but did report the incident to the superintendent.

STOP THE MUSIC!

During the lunch periods in an elementary school, the parent coordinator was asked to play music for the children. A survey of favorite music was taken by the children and given to the parent coordinator, who downloaded the music to play. The music selections were pre-screened by the principal for appropriateness and was edited and censored if required. The parent coordinator played music during both lunch periods, five days a week. Children were also provided opportunities to dance and engage in dance contests where everyone was made to feel like a winner.

During one lunch period, a parent came into the principal's office to say that her child was unable to listen or participate in these musical activities due to religious beliefs. The parent insisted that although he could not stop the school from playing music, he wanted his child to sit outside of the lunchroom to eat while music was being played. The parent coordinator and principal met with the parent immediately. The principal shared that the lunch periods were a great time for socialization. She asked the parent if the child was able to participate in board games or use technology during that time. In collaboration with the parent, Parent-Teacher Association, and assistant principal, stations were set up outside the lunchroom giving children choices of what to do with their time during both lunch periods. The parent was happy and allowed his child to participate by playing games. It was agreed that the child would not go into the lunchroom during music time.

WHAT HAPPENED TO THE BEEF PATTIES?

A parent requested to meet with the principal regarding the food served in the lunchroom. The parent said, "I know that this may be trivial to you, but it is really a big deal to my child. On Thursday, they ran out of beef patties. Apparently, they did not have enough for all of the children. My child had to eat chicken nuggets instead." Needless to say, this was a big issue for the child and mother, as they talked about it the entire day.

The parent wanted to know if there was a way for the principal to make sure that all children had beef patties. She wanted the principal to ensure that enough were ordered and that the kitchen would not run out.

Although she said that chicken nuggets were fine on any other day, it was not acceptable for the kitchen to run out of a particular food that the children looked forward to eating.

The principal assured the parent that she would discuss the issue with the kitchen manager. She also explained that the kitchen staff did their best to make sure that the children selected lunches of their choice. Furthermore, she shared that from time to time, certain selections of food run out. She let the parent know that she would meet with the kitchen manager to find the types of foods kids loved the most, in the hopes that they could order a bit more of those items on special days. The parent left the meeting understanding that similar to any restaurant setting, there could be no guarantee that certain foods would be available on specific days.

CAVIAR ANYONE?

Two private school parents, both physicians, came to the principal's office citing their son's allergy problems. They explained their son is allergic to peanut butter and caviar. They wanted to make sure that the principal understood that caviar was not to be on the lunch menu. The principal politely assured the parents that caviar would not be served in the school cafeteria at any point and time. The parents left feeling happy and assured that their request had been acknowledged. And believe it or not, caviar never appeared on the lunchroom cafeteria menu.

PIZZA ON THE MENU

A parent came to the principal's office complaining about the quality of pizza served in the school cafeteria on Fridays. She said that the pizza at a local popular franchise was tastier. She also mentioned that the pizza was of low quality and wanted the principal to order from a different vendor. The principal listened to the parents' concern for several minutes. After listening quietly, she began to explain how much the children loved pizza Fridays. She explained that the school had served pizza on Fridays for many years, much at the request of the children. The principal said, "I am not questioning your taste buds, but the children really enjoy this pizza. I also am not responsible for food service purchasing. That is the responsibility of the food service dietician. The food is contracted for a year, so the contracted vendor can not be changed". The principal finally informed the parent that Pizza Fridays was not mandatory. She suggested that the child might be happier bringing in lunch from home on those days. The parent was not happy, became irate and quickly walked out of the office. The child was seen happily eating her pizza every Friday at lunch.

THE SHOULDER TOUCH

Children can be so amazingly wonderful, quite rambunctious, and sometimes naughty during the school day. Teachers, support staff, and school administrators all have a responsibility to uphold a safe environment for everyone. However, some children can find ways to be naughty, at best, on a daily basis. In these instances, parents and caregivers are often called to buffer difficult situations when children are fidgety.

Emeril was an energetic seven-year-old child who sometimes experienced great challenges getting through the school day. One day during the lunch period, he decided to walk on tables, throw food, slide under tables, and run aimlessly throughout the room.

After many attempts by the school aides to support him, the principal was called. She walked in, put her hands on his shoulders, and escorted him to her office where the family advocate called his family. Fifteen minutes later, his uncle walked into the school, spouting profanities and shouted, "Where's my nephew?" He tried to rush directly into the principal's office, but was stopped by school security. The family advocate heard the commotion in the hallway and ran to talk to the uncle. She asked him to wait with security for a few moments and she would return to escort him into the office. The advocate ran up the stairs to locate the principal. She asked the principal to remain upstairs because of the uncle's violent nature. She assured the principal that she was very familiar with the uncle and she could calm the situation. With great hesitation, the principal remained on the second floor for some time, in a nervous state.

About an hour later, the advocate called for the principal to come to the first floor. As they sat together in the office, the advocate explained that although it took some convincing, she was able to de-escalate the situation. She explained that the uncle believed that the principal, a white woman, was biased against the needs of a child of color. Although he did not apologize for his disparaging comments toward the principal, he agreed to leave the school without further incident.

A MOTHER'S LOVE

Every day, a parent escorted her four year old child into the school to partake in morning breakfast. Mom would help the child get their tray, sit at a table, and set up their napkins, milk, and spork. It was a perfect table setting for a young child, and mom appeared to enjoy her time as the loving and watchful parent. Once everything was set up, mother sat and cut up the food with precision, while the child sat patiently waiting. Mother then chewed up part of the food and fed it to her child.

Although the children at the table did not appear to notice, the supervisor and school aides did. They spoke with the principal who in turn, discussed the issue with the supervisor. The principal was confused, because children generally sat in for breakfast without parents. How was the mother sitting every day during what should have been an independent and social time for the child? The supervisor explained that she allowed the mother to come in because it was the beginning of the school year. The mother was very anxious, so she was allowed to walk her child in for breakfast. The supervisor admitted that, after a few weeks, it became difficult to get mom to leave. She just did not have the heart to ask her to stop sitting with her child.

Together they discussed how to talk to mom and convince her to leave for the day. The conversation had to be carefully thought out, so as not to insult or upset mom or the child. Salvoney and Mayer (1990) observed wide variations in an individuals' ability to detect others' emotions, understand their own emotions, and use this information to guide their interactions with others. They labeled this ability emotional intelligence. Goleman (2004) highlighted a strong link between emotional intelligence (EI) and leadership ability. Furthermore, he posited EI enables leaders to keep emotions in check, demonstrate rational decision-making, and persuade others by finding common ground.

The next day of school, the supervisor met mom at the entrance of the lunchroom. She greeted her with a warm smile and spoke to her about the issue of her staying during morning breakfast. She told her that beginning on the very next day, her child would enter and eat breakfast on her own. Also, she praised the mother for preparing her child for independence and let her know that her child was completely ready and able to eat without any support. The mother appeared hesitant, nervous, and unsure of what to do. With a mild hug, the supervisor assured her that she had done a wonderful job and that everything would be just fine. Mother set up the table that day as usual. She then sat next to her child, observing and giving directions while the child ate on her own. The child continued eating on her own for the rest of the school year.

SECTION TWO:

School Bus Escorts and Class Trips

INTRODUCTION

The yellow school bus has been transporting children to markets, theaters, and museums for decades. Everyone recognizes the oddly shaped bus as an indication that children are somewhere about. In schools across the country, children frolic onto these vehicles in anticipation of the thrill that awaits them at the end of the ride. They spend time tossing their bags, throwing food, and in a few joyous moments learn to socialize in ways that only children can.

School trips turn a regular school day into a magnificent outdoor experience. Children board the bus to escape the sometimes repetitive nature of the school day for an adventurous ride that brings classroom learning to life. These buses provide children transportation to places that boast an endless cycle of wonder, inquiry, and exploration. Without question, the bus is special, offering students the opportunity to visit the zoo, seaports, clay pits, and other destinations that challenge their imaginations. Trips broaden a child's cognitive development, allowing them to deconstruct and make sense of newly acquired information from the world around them.

A school trip can be arranged by the teacher to reinforce what was taught in class and help students understand the topic better. Many times these excursions enable students to see new sites that enhance their lives. This can be particularly helpful for students who are less fortunate and do not have the opportunity to travel.

In many classrooms across the world, parents are encouraged to escort children on trips. This is a great time for parents to see first-hand what their child may be learning in class. They also get a chance to see how their child interacts with their teacher and peers in these social situations. The teacher may request a few parent escorts, or sometimes allow one parent for each child depending on the trip. Parents are an essential part of trips because they help keep the entire class community safe. These field trips are an exciting element of every child's learning experience.

The following stories are some of the adventures that have taken place during scheduled class trips.

THE CASE OF THE MISSING HAIRPIECE

It was a class trip nightmare. A teacher was taking her third grade class on a trip to the zoo and she asked parents to join the trip as chaperones. Parents were told to meet the bus at nine in the morning in front of the school on the morning of the trip. At around five after nine, shortly after the bus pulled away from the school, a mother who was to be a chaperone on the trip was seen running down the street, yelling at the bus driver to stop the bus. She was screaming at him to let her on the bus, as she was supposed to be a chaperone on her daughter's class trip.

When the parent stepped onto the bus she was dressed in a fancy outfit, wearing lots of make-up and an elaborate hairdo. Some time during the trip, the parent noticed her hair piece was missing. The class teacher called the principal to say that the parent lost her hair piece and was crying hysterically. She asked the principal for suggestions about what she should do.

The principal told the teacher to ask the parent to board the bus so they could return to school on time. The parent refused to get back on the bus until her hairpiece was found. The teacher and the students retraced their steps, looking for the hairpiece. Finally, after more than an hour, someone found the hairpiece lying next to an animal's cage. The parent was greatly relieved and quickly boarded the bus to get back home. When the class returned to school, the principal told the teacher that this parent was never to be invited on a class trip again, as there was no need for any future hairy moments.

ESCORT CHALLENGES

A kindergarten class took a trip to the museum in early January. Several parents were asked to accompany the children on the trip for added safety. While on the school bus, one child began jumping around, yelling out randomly, and talking loudly to the child sitting next to him. The teacher walked over to the child several times while the bus was en route. However, the child continued to distract many of the other children on the bus. The teacher was also active at making sure that all of the children were safe.

When the bus returned to the school following the trip, a group of parents went into the main office and demanded to speak with the principal. The parents said they felt that the child should not attend any more trips. They were willing to go to the superintendent's office to ask for the child to be removed from all future trips. They believed that he was emotionally challenged, disruptive, and difficult to manage on the bus. The principal met with the parents and listened to their concerns. She explained that field trips were an important part of the learning process for all children.She asked them to keep in mind that kindergarten children were learning how to understand the world around them, including their interactions with their peers. They were also learning how to navigate new experiences through experiential learning opportunities provided by the school.

The principal continued explaining that part of exploring the world meant that teachers, paraprofessionals, and parents are escorts to support the entire class during trips. This meant that the teacher may need to support one child slightly more while he or she adjusts to taking field trips. She helped them understand that the role of parent escorts was essential in assisting the teacher with maintaining a safe and orderly experience for the children. She assured the parents that the child was simply becoming accustomed to new experiences and that time would settle him or her down completely. She then thanked them for attending the trip and for being so observant and caring toward the children. Emotional intelligence research suggests effective leadership is an everyday event that requires the "ability to communicate, listen intently, and maintain a considerate disposition that builds trust and understanding" (Maudling, et al., 2012 p 25). The parents continued to act as escorts on future trips. No other student concerns were brought to the teacher or principal.

CLASS TRIP DISAPPEARING PARENT

The parents of a student who had social and behavioral issues received a call from the principal. They were informed that their child could not attend a class trip to the aquarium unless an adult accompanied him. The mother wanted her child to go so she agreed to escort her child.

Upon arriving at their destination the teacher gave parents directions about how to support children while on the trip. She also was specific about the time the bus would leave at 11:30 a.m. going back to the school. While giving each child a partner and taking a head count, the parent took off without her son. The teacher was shocked but knew that she had to continue guiding the class through the exhibits.

At 11:30 a.m., the class was fully boarded on the bus, but the parent was nowhere in sight. The teachers and bus driver were furious and wanted to leave her behind. The teacher called the principal and was told to do everything they could to find her. Finally, about two hours after the agreed departure time, the parent appeared. Her child was so angry that he started yelling and kicking her. The bus driver and a teacher had to intervene. When they arrived back at the school, the bus driver escorted them to the principal's office.

The administrator reminded the mother that she was on the trip to attend to the behavioral needs of her son. Upon hearing that, the mother became very angry and began to hurl expletives at the principal. She also informed the principal that she would never go on a school trip again. The school leader was so flabbergasted by her behavior he just let her leave the office in a huff.

THE CASE OF THE TRAVELING GRANDMOTHER

It was customary for the sixth, seventh, and eighth grade middle school students of one school to take a three-day overnight trip to Boston, Philadelphia, or Washington, D.C. While it was always fun, it also had its challenges of keeping the students in line, getting them to stay in their rooms and go to sleep, and, most notably, moving them along during the day to make sure that they got to see everything that was scheduled on the itinerary. One year, a young girl who had a number of physical as well as cognitive challenges was along on the trip.

While she was mainstreamed academically, she still required individual care. One of her parents was required to accompany her on a class trip. This plan worked fine until one year when her mom couldn't make it and insisted that she would send Grandma to care for the student. Mom insisted that Grandma had lots of energy and often cared for the girl at home. The principal was not happy about the parent's insistence, but under pressure the principal reluctantly agreed. It turned out to be not the principal's best decision. Grandma was not warm and fuzzy. She questioned everything. She was particularly concerned and critical about the meals on the trip, as they were not quite up to her standards. Amazingly, her granddaughter was able to keep up with the class, but Grandma was always way behind.

On the second day of the trip, as the group walked around Boston Commons, an uneven piece of sidewalk did Grandma in. She fell, hitting her head and scraping her knee. The student became hysterical seeing Grandma in pain and an ambulance was summoned. The parents and staff who were accompanying the group worried about what might possibly happen to Grandma.

Miraculously, Grandma's injuries turned out to be fairly superficial. The ambulance crew cleaned her wounds and bandaged them. She refused to go to the hospital and managed to get back on her feet, now even more wobbly than before. The supervising teacher consulted with her daughter (the student's mom) and decided that she would remain with the group until the end of the trip, but would stay on the bus for most of the remaining stops. Everyone survived and the group returned to school the next evening with a great sigh of relief.

THE FIFTY-DOLLAR PARENT HOSTAGE

Students in the second grade take a trip to the Bronx Zoo each spring. One year, a parent who went with her child on the trip to chaperone did not arrive at the designated time of departure. The teacher called the security office and was told that the parent was being held at the gift shop, as she had stolen items from the shop and they required fifty dollars before releasing her. The parent said she did not have the money, and the items were junk and not worth the money they were charging. Afraid that the zoo was going to call the police, the teachers and parents on the trip pooled their money to pay her debt. The parent was then allowed to leave and boarded the bus back to the school. The principal met the bus when it arrived at the school and asked the parent to come into the office to discuss the matter. The principal explained calmly and respectfully that stealing from the gift shop would jeopardize the school being able to ever take students to the zoo again. Upon hearing what the principal said, the parent walked out without saying a word.

SECTION THREE:

Parent Requests

INTRODUCTION

It may come as a surprise to many folks, but the principal is the " it" person. This means that as an administrator, the principal is responsible for everything that happens within the walls of their school. Although there is a trend to have parents actively involved in decision-making in the schools, the principal is the one who ultimately makes the final decision. Along with the assistant principal, they will respond to issues, concerns, and emergencies within the school. And everyone who comes to the main office wants a seat at the principal's table.

Bennis (2007) states: "…you must trust yourself, that you be self-directed rather than other directed in your work. If you learn to anticipate the future and shape events rather than being shaped by them, you will benefit in significant ways." (p 71)

This summarizes how a leader needs to be prepared to deal with many different situations.

Most parents, teachers, and outsiders have no idea how many situations a principal has to navigate on a daily basis. Successful principals are exceptionally skillful practitioners who must learn to make quick, smart, and realistic decisions, sometimes based only on limited information. Yet, there are times when they have an opportunity to think about things before they reach a final decision. There is no doubt that the role of being a principal is huge, probably much bigger than the public realizes. The principalship entails constant self-reflection about the decisions they are ultimately charged to make. Bennis (2009) posits "Listening to the inner voice—trusting the inner voice—is one of the most important lessons of leadership" (p 29).

In a proficient professional learning community, a principal will build trust by collaborating with teachers and parents for different reasons. They will meet with teachers for conferences, grade level meetings, curriculum planning, and classroom observation discussions. Parents are members of a number of teams in the school: leadership team, PTA, safety, hiring, and other committees that are needed to create a warm and safe learning environment. However, in spite of all of this democracy, by the end of the school year, a principal has made a multitude of decisions, either collectively or independently, that impact their school community. And at the end of the road, they are also the primary defenders of any and all decisions made for the school, even when they are in collaboration with parents and teachers.

Being a principal or school administrator is not an easy position to hold. Regardless of how hard a principal may try, it is extremely difficult to make all parents and teachers feel special or satisfied about any final decisions the school leader has deemed to be the right choice for their school community. Although there are times when there is great appreciation, respect, and validation for the hard work that principals do, there are also many moments of discontent. Because of this, principals must develop a strong sense of self in order to manage the hurtful social media posts and angry phone calls attached to the position. With so much to learn, so many decisions to make, and so many people to please, what is a principal to do? In the book A Simpler Way, the authors posit, "When simple relationships are created, patterns of organizations emerge" (Wheatley & Kellner-Rogers, 1999, p 32).

While creating these relationships, having conversations, and developing safe spaces for the staff and parents to discuss and air their concerns, the principal designs a culture within the school. A tone is set that implies all are welcome and the principal's door is open for all school community members at all times. Schein (2010) viewed these types of conversations as "cultural islands," emphasizing the need for people to create settings for casual conversations that lead to problem solving and shared decision-making. Who supports and protects the principal? How many times will a principal hear loving terms of endearment and sheer appreciation with the simple phrase "Job well done"? But that is not at the heart of what matters most to the school leader. It is the satisfaction that emanates from within that the principal's decision will positively affect the students. The following stories are examples of just some of the parent requests that principals navigate throughout the year.

MAY WE HAVE A NEW
TEACHER, PLEASE?

A parent representative from a grade sixth class made an appointment to speak with the principal during the month of July. The parent began the conversation by stating that she and a group of parents had met privately to discuss concerns about the teacher slated to teach their special class for the upcoming year. The children in this particular class move up in cohorts.

Although the children had the teacher in fifth grade, they were scheduled to have her once again for sixth grade.

The parents made a collective decision that they wanted an alternate teacher to teach the class. The parents believed that although the teacher had a pleasant personality, she was a second-year teacher who had experienced difficulty communicating, struggled with organization, and produced test results lower than expected for the class. The representative informed the principal that if the teacher remained in the position for the upcoming year, the parents were prepared to take their children out of the school. In the following weeks, other parents requested to meet with the principal, all sharing their concerns regarding the placement of the teacher. They also shared that as a body of parents, they would be forced to find other schools for the children. They insisted that the decision to leave the school would be directly related to their strong belief that the teacher could not provide their children with the support needed to yield adequate academic performance. They asked the principal to highly consider their request for an alternate teacher, as they did not believe that two years with an inadequate teacher would best serve their children.

The principal told the parents that during the summer, assignments often shift due to staff transfers to different schools or relocation opportunities. She explained that she would not like to see parents leave the school, but those choices were individual and independent of teacher placement. The principal informed the parents that she understood the concerns of the families and thanked them for expressing their ideas. She also let them know that teacher assignments were made at the discretion of the principal in collaboration with the teacher. She asked the parents to trust that the final decision would be made in the best interest of all children. Without sharing the intricacies of the parent meetings, the principal phoned the classroom teacher to discuss her feelings about the current school year. The teacher shared that the preceding year had been challenging in terms of organization, management, and numerous parent issues.

Following a conversation with the assistant principal and observations of the teacher's practice from the previous year, it was determined that the teacher would experience greater success on an alternate grade level. Ultimately, the children also entered the school year with a more seasoned teacher. The teacher was more than willing to shift her assignment, as the previous year had been relatively difficult. As a result, the teacher and principal agreed that she would be placed in a third grade assignment. This amicable decision allowed the principal to hire a new teacher for the new six grade class.

ICT IS NOT FOR MY CHILD

During the second week of school, a parent came into the school very upset that her child was registered in an Integrated Co-Teaching classroom. She demanded that her child be taken out of the setting, because she believed that the child would not make adequate progress. The parent requested a meeting with the classroom teacher and the parent coordinator. The parent insisted that her child would not benefit academically by sitting in a class with children with disabilities. Although the teacher tried to explain the benefits of the class, particularly for her child, the parent became upset. There was no resolution to the problem and the parent was not pleased with the outcome of the discussion. Subsequently, the parent requested a meeting with the principal, teacher and parent coordinator.

A group meeting was arranged the next school day. During the meeting, the parent was given a copy of the final report card from the previous year. A letter was sent home informing the parent of the new class placement. The classroom teacher from the previous school year also met with the parent to discuss the ICT class. Both the parent and teacher agreed that her child would perform well with two teachers in the class.

After carefully discussing the child's assessment and current academic performance, the teacher told the parent that her child was performing well. The teacher explained that the child would have opportunities to work in smaller groups. This would provide her with healthy discussions with her peers and social interactions with her peers.

The benefits of the class were further explained, as the class had two exceptional teachers with a ratio of ten children to one teacher. The parent was asked to allow her child to attend the class for two more weeks. If there was no evidence that the child was progressing, then they would reevaluate the placement. The child performed extremely well during that time, as well as for the remainder of the year in the Integrated Co-Teaching setting. Leithwood et al (2004) stated the school leader's most noteworthy contributions impact student learning (p 13). It is important to remember that student learning is the principal's major focus and responsibility. Ultimately, the decision to have the child remain in the ICT class was an appropriate placement for that student.

STUDENT CLASS TRANSFER CONCERNS

During the month of November, a class representative of a sixth grade high-performing class requested an appointment to meet with the principal. The parent entered the principal's office and took out an agenda of concerns from the parents of the class. The parent suggested that the teacher was experiencing difficulty acclimating to the new school environment. The teacher was unorganized, appeared to lack focus, and offered students limited support as a whole in the classroom. They were also concerned that several of the parents requested that their children be placed in a different sixth grade class. This resulted in the class having fewer students, which the parents believed limited student academic discussion and, ultimately, student learning. The parent implied that it would be catastrophic to the school if parents decided to simply leave the school because of a struggling new teacher. She asked the principal if there was something that could be done to provide the new teacher with more support so families would stop asking for transfers to alternate classrooms.

The principal thanked the parent for sharing her concerns. She also informed the parent that transfer requests were private and therefore could not be discussed. She also informed the parent that the discussion of any teacher, challenges or not, would be a professional breach of confidentiality. Therefore, she was not willing to engage in that particular conversation. However, she did assure the parent that all teachers in the school, including her child's teacher, were highly qualified to teach the class to which they were assigned. The principal also told the parent that, as per the standards set forth by the state, all teachers were actively participating in professional enhancement programs, including mentoring for all new teachers. The principal assured the parent that the school administration was actively supporting and monitoring all new teachers to ensure the best academic outcomes for all students. The parent left the meeting with an uneasy sense of resolve. Yet, she agreed to the idea that the school administrators would monitor both the teacher performance and children's progress.

As the year progressed, the teacher experienced ongoing challenges from poor management, lack of planning, and difficulty working in teams across the grade. Students complained to the principal on numerous occasions that they were simply not learning. By the spring of the school year, there had been several meetings and disciplinary conferences with the union to discuss the teacher's poor performance. As a result, the teacher was asked not to return to the school for the subsequent school year.

SUNSHINE PLEASE

One day the lunchroom supervisor reported to the principal that a third grade student's mother came in to see where her daughter was seated in the lunchroom. She informed the lunchroom supervisor that the seat her daughter was seated in was not acceptable. The supervisor told the mother she would have to discuss the matter with the principal. The mother came up to the principal's office that afternoon and said her daughter must sit next to the window, as she needed to have her daily dose of sunshine. The principal explained that students are to sit with their classmates, as social interaction with peers is an important part of the school day. The mother would not take no for an answer and continued to repeat that her daughter must sit right next to the window. The principal listened and, once again, said that for safety reasons the child must sit with her classmates. The mother could not or would not accept the principal's response and came every day for a week trying to change her daughter's seat. Her daughter finally told the mother that she wanted to sit with her classmates and to stop embarrassing her. That seemed to work, as the mother stopped visiting with her daughter at lunch.

THE WRONG SEX

A mother came to see the principal, explaining that she and her husband were very upset about her son's first-grade class placement. The principal asked what was wrong with the placement. The parents believed that a man should not teach first grade, because they are not nurturing. Therefore, they wanted a female teacher. They also insisted that he should be fired or, at the very least, their child should be taken off the class roster. The principal clearly told the mother he was a fine teacher who would be able to understand and meet her son's educational needs. As the principal, she hoped that the parents would agree that the school was doing everything they could to educate her son. A few months later, they withdrew their son from the school because the principal did not adhere to their demands.

THE END OF HOMEWORK, PLEASE!

A parent of a second grade student came in to discuss the school homework policy with the teacher and principal. There were several issues that were discussed, including disagreeing with the idea of homework as a whole. The parent stated that research completely disagreed with the notion of giving children homework. She proceeded to provide articles supporting her claim. The parent disagreed with homework being a part of an early childhood daily schedule. Yet, she was willing to discuss the time factors and quality of homework that was being sent home. Additionally, the parent shared that her child was involved in a number of extra-curricular activities: art class, swimming, karate, Spanish classes, and woodworking, making it extremely difficult for the child to attend these activities without the worry of homework. The parent also cited that homework interfered with family time at home.

The principal met with both the parent and teacher to take a closer look at the assignments for the second grade. It was clear that the family had many activities outside of the regular school day. However, the teacher informed the parent that, just as in life, the class had expectations for the completion of assignments. After looking at the homework, it was clear that it was a reinforcement of the days lesson. The assignments were not extensive enough to interfere with the family's quality of life. The teacher and principal expressed the importance of supporting children through the process of learning. They shared that the home–school connection was a fabulous way of connecting parents to the work their children were doing in class. At the same time, children were learning to complete assignments, including some forms of world research that were relevant to class units of study. The parent disagreed, citing that her preference was no homework at all. The school informed the parent of the homework policy and let the parents know that in the school they selected, families were expected to comply, with some flexibility, to the policy.

WARM WALLS

One day, a father came to the principal's office demanding that the walls of his son's classroom be changed immediately. His son's kindergarten classroom was painted in primary colors: red, yellow, and blue. When asked why he had this request, the father explained his son did not like these colors and became overly stimulated in the classroom. He insisted that the room be repainted in pastel colors over the weekend. The principal said that this could not be done over the weekend, but would think about the possibility of repainting the room in more subdued colors for the following year. The father said nothing, but stormed out of the office. He never came back with another paint request the rest of the year.

THE PERFECT CHILDREN IN A PERFECT CLASS

Children of all kinds account for the beauty in every classroom. In this school, children were children and the principal loved them all regardless of race, creed, religious affiliation, or color. In some classrooms in large cities, special classrooms are designated for children with special needs or those with exceptional qualities. Regardless of either, it is the children who shape and mold the dynamics of the class. Together they build a sense of unity and uniqueness and learn to respect the boundaries and space for all.

One of the classes had about eighteen students enrolled. It was relatively equally mixed between boys and girls. The children were smart, inquisitive, and rambunctious, just as young children are in all classrooms. Yet, it happened that one child stood out above the rest. He was just as bright, beautiful, and rambunctious as the rest of the children, and then he began having multiple disagreements or spats with some of his classmates. These situations were nothing unusual, but for parents in the room, it did not fit their model of the way an exceptional child should behave. So, the year progressed with this little fellow learning how to make his way through not only social situations but also working through a classroom environment grounded in perceived perfection.

Midway through the year, parents decided that they would gather to discuss a solution to what they thought was a class problem. In their minds, he did not belong in the class. He was too loud, too rough, larger than the other children, and far more boisterous than the other children. The families believed that he did not fit into the class structure and wanted him removed. They worked together to try to persuade the principal to place him into another class. The parents in this community had an open door policy to the local district office. They let the principal know that they would use their relationship with the district staff to get the child removed from the class, yet implored the principal to make that decision on her own.

Given the belief that children need time to develop, build relationships, and simply grow into wonderful people, the principal did not concede to their idea of removing the child. Yes, he was bigger than the other children, boisterous, rough, and sometimes loud. But, he was also sweet, loving, and, most of all, super smart. He was not removed from the class and, after parents spent another year of trying to have him removed to no avail, things eventually began to settle down. It was a great day when he proudly walked across the graduation stage. He shared that perfect day with the children he had grown to know and love over the years. He needed time to mature and develop into the fine young man that he is today. It was never the children who wanted him out of the class, it was always their parents. Hopefully, the parents grew to understand that there is no such thing as a perfect child or a perfect class.

SECTION FOUR:

Perceived Indiscretions, Rumors, Drinks, and Fun Times

INTRODUCTION

There is truth in the phrase, "Old perceptions die hard!" particularly when it comes to the role of leadership. Both novice and senior administrators listen to a barrage of stories, complaints, and concerns regularly. They become relatively skillful in learning how to decipher the truth from fiction. Often they receive information from their community that they did not elicit. These on-going circumstances create a quagmire of difficult situations that rest in the laps of school leaders.

How do rumors, old perceptions, blogs, and ridiculous complaints impact on the reputation of school leaders and other staff? How does a school leader navigate parties and other staff events and continue to supervise staff in an effective manner? When do school leaders cross the boundaries of leadership and sail off into the waters of inappropriate behavior? How does a principal filter through staff complaints to determine fact from fiction?

The cognitive process of leadership is complex. There is no simple way for a school leader to work through difficult situations. However, it is especially precarious when issues involve indiscretions by staff members. There is no question that a large amount of our time is spent at work. We develop relationships with many people including parents, teachers, and students. However, as school leaders, it is important for us to understand that we are public servants and, as such, we have a professional and moral obligation to do our best to remain fair, right, and just. Because of this, it is essential to understand how critical it is to refrain from acting on rumors, public blogs, or acting inappropriately at a staff party. One act of indiscretion can change how people view school leaders. The public holds school leaders at a high moral standard. As a result, there is little room for leadership errors of any kind. The consequences of a mistake can be disastrous and lead to disciplinary actions, including termination of employment.

BOTTOMS UP

As part of the winter holiday vacation, several staff members of a school met at a local pub to share some memories, drinks, and laughs. Although the invitation was not open to all staff, the assistant principal of the school was asked to join the group. During their time at the pub, they all drank from moderate to heavy portions. After several drinks and shots, the assistant principal began to share details of his personal life with the teachers. This included the problems that he was having with his wife, as well as his admiration for his current mistress. As if that was not enough, he made sure that the staff understood that they needed to keep their discussions private so the principal did not get wind of anything. Upon returning to school for the new semester, the incident was brought to the attention of the principal.

Since the incident took place after school hours, the principal considered much of it as hearsay. When asked if the teachers were willing to put it in writing they refused, so it was not reported as misconduct. However, the principal did inform the assistant principal that a complaint had been brought to his attention. The principal suggested to the assistant principal that he may want to reconsider going out for drinks with the staff that he supervised. He was also warned to be mindful of the appropriateness of his discussions in and outside of the school community. The principal also told the assistant principal that he could not guarantee that one of the other teachers would not report the incident to the investigation department as professional misconduct.

THE MENTOR HECKLER

Often, new principals will ask seasoned administrators their opinions about a particular situation in their school or to act as a sounding board for them. It is a way to clarify thinking and perhaps become aware of a best practice that had not been formerly considered. Sometimes they are called mentors and actually spend time in the building with the new principal to act as another set of ears or eyes and give another perspective on a situation or practice the new principal is thinking of implementing. However, the staff of this school was not accustomed to a principal conducting frequent walkthroughs. Mr. Harold P. Chowder (pseudonym) was the new principal of this challenging and low-performing school. He immediately wanted to become familiar with overall routines as well as learn the culture of the building.

In late September, Principal Chowder introduced his assigned mentor, Ms. Sharel, to the staff at a faculty meeting. Principal Chowder explained the role of the mentor, which was to assist him in various supervisory areas. He also explained that Ms. Sharel would not evaluate teachers. Her role was solely to evaluate the principal.

It so happened that Mr. Bromwell, a senior teacher who did not have classroom responsibilities, took offense that a mentor for the new principal would be allowed in his building. So, Mr. Bromwell waited for Ms. Sharel outside the school building one day. Mr. Bromwell was rude, loud, and almost verbally abusive to Ms. Sharel. He chastised her, with a warning that she was not welcome in the school. He did this in front of parents and students who were being dismissed.

The next day the incident was reported to Mr. Chowder by several parents and teachers. He spoke with Ms. Sharel and she confirmed that the incident had taken place. She was insulted and embarrassed by the incident. Principal Chowder called Mr. Bromwell and asked him to come to the office for a conversation. Of course, Mr. Bromwell told a version which was very different from that of Ms. Sharel. Both recalled the situation in completely different ways.

Mr. Bromwell said, "That never happened." Principal Chowder did not believe this to be the truth, given that several other people had individually reported witnessing what Ms. Sharel described. The quandary was how to follow up and control the situation so that it did not fester in the school environment? Mr. Chowder decided to let it play out, which turned out not to be the best decision.

Mr. Bromwell ultimately went to the union representative to question the validity of the principal having Ms. Sharel walking into classrooms with Principal Chowder. Although the union assured him that this practice was within the scope of an administrator's role, this began a series of 311 calls, (311 is a complaint hotline), about every new action taken by the

Principal Chowder to improve the teaching and learning practices in this school. This made it harder to implement new practices with the senior staff. Eventually he was able to hire new staff, either through retirement or attrition. Over time, the menacing calls began to subside. Soon after, Mr. Bromwell retired and the complaint calls came to a screeching halt.

When Principal Chowder retired several years later, he received a special telegram from Mr. Bromwell. In it he wrote, "Mr. Chowder, congratulations on your retirement! I am having a blast and hope that you, too, will enjoy the next chapter of your life. I hope that you will be just as happy as I am." Mr. Chowder wondered, Is Mr. Bromwell really happy, or is he just being a menace even in my retirement?

SECTION FIVE:

Smelly Situations

INTRODUCTION

What is a principal to do when uncertain of how to address a smelly situation? The principal asks, inquires, and digs deep deciding how to have that uncomfortable discussion about … things that smell!

Most principals have encountered situations that required them to shield or discuss the importance of maintaining confidentiality for conversations that they are forced to have. It's not just about teachers who may need support, but also situations with children and ancillary staff.

How does a principal clear up unhealthy situations? The reality is that as the leader, they are forced to ensure the safety and well-being of all members of the community. Subsequently, they must wear the hat of judge and jury. Because when things get smelly in a school building, not a single person wants to be the one to say something or someone stinks!

POOR HI-GENE

A school is filled with blends of scents from adolescent children, school lunch, smelly bathrooms, and a host of other sniffles. One of the most challenging smells to deal with is that of a co-worker who has an unpleasant odor. The smell from one of their colleagues began to emerge slowly over the course of three years. Complaints started to surface from not only children but also from classroom teachers as well.

During the reorganization of classrooms sometime in early May, two teachers met with the principal to ask specifically not to work with the particular employee. One expressed that the smell was so bad that it filled the room and made him physically sick. It so happened that the employee stopped by to see the principal in June. To her surprise, she could barely stand to sit in the room with him. She thought to herself, How in the world am I going to help this person? How do I tell someone that they are in need of hygiene support? Why is this my responsibility? Is it my responsibility? The reality was that at that point, the entire school community was whispering about the stench. What was a principal to do? So many questions crossed the mind of the principal. Was this person involved in some kind of initiation into a college sorority? Was it a cultural belief of some kind? Was it simply an issue of poor hygiene? Whatever the case, the principal wasn't sure if this stinky situation fell within the guidelines of administration. Nevertheless, she knew that it was affecting many people in the school, most of all the children. With great reluctance, she had a very tactful and sensitive discussion after school with the employee, who was unaware of his own scent.

SOMETHING STINKS

It is inevitable that challenges with facilities happen throughout the school year. Issues as simple as peeling paint or broken locks to more challenging and dangerous situations like broken water fountains and falling ceiling tiles are just some of the problems that a principal has to deal with daily.

One day in April, students were celebrating Poetry Month. Traditionally, students studied different forms and styles of poetry and experimented with different strategies such as free verse, haiku, rhyme, onomatopoeia, and alliteration. Lots of preparation was needed to be ready for the Poetry Slam, the culmination of the celebration. Students collaborated on creating original work, the multi-purpose space was decorated with curtains, and round tables were set up with fancy tablecloths and fake candles. Large signs were posted outside the school weeks ahead announcing the event and snacks were purchased for families attending the special celebration. Fourth and fifth graders from the school's band rehearsed and prepared for added entertainment to compliment the Poetry Slam.

Guests were welcomed, and there was a full house of happy families and nervous students. The presentation began with wonderful introductions and beautiful poetry recited or read by students. At about the sixth poem, something smelled funny, literally.

The night before the celebration, there was a heavy rainstorm, but there was no hint of what was to follow the next morning. During the Poetry Slam, the boiler room, located adjacent to the multi-purpose room, began to spew sewage water from behind its doors. The water was seen first, and then the smell identified it! Poop! Guests were disgusted and students were horrified. On their worst day, no one would have ever imagined this. The custodial engineer was called, the room evacuated, and guests were relocated to the school library on the third floor. Students went back to their classrooms with their teachers. The celebration continued in the library, with groups of students listed in the booklet called from their classrooms since not everyone could be accommodated in the library at the same time.

The following day, the principal sent a letter to the school community explaining what had transpired and what steps were taken to address the problem. The district's facilities manager was notified, and a team was sent to further address the problem. That particular Poetry Slam was a memorable day!

I HAVE TO GO

Instant gratification is a given with very young children, whether it be a reward for good behavior or an expressed need. They just can't wait for too long, and this is certainly understandable as they are socially and emotionally in the Me Stage developmentally. So, it comes as no surprise when a conflict arises between two five-year olds when their needs aren't met immediately.

Two kindergarteners boys were caught up in a disagreement because they both had to use the bathroom. The restroom had recently been renovated to make it meet the requirements for students with special needs. Where two stalls and two urinals had been there previously, the new bathroom now contained only one stall and two urinals for approximately thirty, five-year old boys.

Danny was already in the stall taking care of business when Mike rushed into the bathroom with his own emergency that could not be satisfied by using the urinal.

Mike knocked on the stall door only to hear Danny respond, "I'm using the bathroom."

"But I have to go!!" Mike shouted. From behind the stall door, Danny yelled, "I have to poop!"

Impatient and uncomfortable, Mike crawled under the stall door only to get a swift kick on the head. Mike ran back to his classroom to complain to the teacher. Danny returned to his classroom to complain to his teacher. Mike was sent to the nurse and had no serious injuries.

That afternoon at dismissal, the teachers explained to the parents of both boys what had transpired. Danny's mom was upset that his privacy was violated, but understood that the other boy had an emergency and, after all, he is only five years old. Mike's mom, on the other hand, was angry that her son was attacked.

That evening during parent–teacher conferences and the annual book sale, the parents had a heated argument in the school hallway in the presence of other parents, guardians, and students. Danny's mom hurled expletives at Mike's mom while her son looked on. The other adults watched and one bystander rushed into the main office to get an administrator to assist. Mike's mom was reminded that she was in a school and that children were listening to her every word, especially her son. This only brought out more anger and more disgusting expletives targeted at bystanders, administrators, and the added threat of calling the police.

Danny's mom was brought into the main office with her children. Mike's mom continued to curse in the school hallway. Other adult members of Mike's family joined in. A conflict between two kindergarteners having the same bathroom needs quickly escalated into a full-blown, unsavory scene that left many shaking their heads. How could this have gone so wrong so quickly?

After parent–teacher conferences ended that evening and everyone had left, the principal met briefly with the parent coordinator and asked her to call both parents the following morning before the school day began to set up separate meetings with each of them in order to get a clearer picture of what had transpired and to assist in resolving the conflict.

It was established that the boys had an on-going conflict from a playground disagreement in the past and this event only exacerbated an already tense relationship. The classroom teachers were made aware of this and were asked to carefully supervise the students on the playground. The school aides were also informed and were asked to engage both boys in positive play experiences during the recess period. The guidance counselor was apprised of the situation and with the parents' permission, met with both kindergarten boys for a couple of counseling sessions.

PUT THE DOORS BACK

At one middle school, the stall doors in the boys' bathrooms were removed since the boys were using the bathrooms to hide and engage in pranks. One day, the mother of a fifth-grade student came into the principal's office demanding the doors to the individual stalls be returned. The principal explained why the doors had been removed, but the mother kept demanding the doors be returned. Upon careful questioning, the mother explained her son felt very uncomfortable seeing his classmates urinating in front of him. He also felt that the boys were watching him. The principal agreed to have one stall with a door put in the upstairs bathroom. The mother reluctantly agreed to the compromise.

TIME TO POTTY

In many classrooms, children ask to use the bathroom quite frequently. Usually those students are escorted to a bathroom or walk with a partner for safety purposes. Most schools require a bathroom procedure and teachers generally adhere to that requirement. That is, except one day when the rules were not followed and things went wrong.

A student informed the classroom school aide that he needed to use the bathroom. For some reason, the aide decided to take the child to a corner of the school yard to urinate in a milk container. This did not seem to be the first incident of its kind, since the teacher and several of the children were aware that this was occurring. The principal requested that the assistant principal notify the parents of the incident. As per protocol, the principal notified her immediate supervisor. All parties involved or those who had knowledge of the incident were also interviewed and disciplined accordingly.

SECTION SIX:

Principal Fears and Unintended Consequences

INTRODUCTION

Consensus and collaboration are an important part of creating a cohesive school environment. Decisions are made through a collaborative process that includes teachers, students, and parents. Many people believe that this structure builds a school community that is democratic in nature. It also ensures that all constituents are valued and have an opportunity to share their ideas, visions, and voices in multiple pockets of the school.

Although there are many opinions that help to shape the vision of a school, the ultimate decisions belong to the principal.

Many people may not be aware that regardless of how the principal makes a decision, even through consensus and collaboration, they are fully responsible for the outcome. This is a very precarious place to be, yet it is a large part of the life of leadership. While it may be easy for those who participated in the process of collaborating in a group with the principal to walk away, the principal must stand tall. Often times, unpopular decisions made by the principal can cause adverse reactions with the community as well.

In almost all cases, the principal will make, and stand by, a decision that benefits the entire school community. However, there are instances when the decisions may cause some members of the school to be annoyed. Parents and caregivers have been known to threaten or harm a principal for a variety of reasons. Imagine how an administrator must feel being threatened with bodily harm by a member of their community. Make no mistake, there are times when a principal may even second guess themselves for a situation that they did not realize was a problem in the first place.

Given the comprehensive nature of the job, it is important for people to simply be a bit kinder, gentler, and more understanding. When things appear to be falling apart, know that a principal will always stand tall for every child in their care. They are undoubtedly some of the golden pillars of the earth.

WATCH YOUR BACK

A newly appointed principal had a disagreement with a parent due to the dismissal of a school employee who happened to be her relative. The parent began coming to the principal repeatedly using vulgar and very threatening language. On one visit, the parent told the principal that she was going to wait for her outside in front of her car. She then told her that she was going to douse her with gasoline and set her on fire. She told the principal, "All you do is sit in your office and entertain men!" She also called the school regularly, cursing at anyone who answered the phone. The parent's tone became more disturbing and the principal began to have unsettled feelings.

On one occasion, two of the principal's tires were slashed, causing a blow out while she was driving home on an expressway. She had strong suspicions who had tampered with the car and was happy to live through the ordeal. She was afraid, and wasn't sure what she should do. In an effort to protect herself, she first had family members pick her up after work for a few weeks. She made an official police report, which was kept on file. She also made her school safety agent aware of the threats. Following a discussion with the legal department, she mailed the parent a limited access letter, which prevented the parent from having access to the school. She notified her superintendent and the school safety director. After a few months, the visits and phone calls ceased.

RELENTLESS BLOGGERS

A third-year principal hosted a meeting to discuss programs for next school year and the on-going vision of the school. All community members were invited to attend the meeting. Together the community ate, drank, and worked together for several hours, trying to decide on new programs and community-based organizations that would support all children. After three hours, one parent became very angry. He jumped up from the table screaming that the principal was not listening to his ideas and that he just couldn't work with the principal. He started to berate the principal openly, tossing his head back and forth. The principal tried to speak with him, but he was almost uncontrollable. He swung open the door and walked out of the room. Needless to say, the principal was shocked, not knowing why he was so angry or, for that matter, what the principal had done.

Upon entering school the next day, the principal saw a group of parents gathered in the lobby. The principal had no idea what was happening. Then one of the parents informed the principal that a blog post had been written the previous night that was highly critical of the principal. The parents were there to prepare the principal for what had been written. The principal walked into the office and together they went on the site to see what had been written. The principal was stunned and her heart sank! Not only had he written unflattering, derogatory things about her as a leader, he also wrote vile things about her as a person. Disgusted, the principal sat in silence for a few minutes. As the group read, it seemed that more parents had joined the blog that morning. Some were defending the principal while others agreed with what the parent had written. The principal believed they were working as a collaborative team, giving all members a voice in the planning process and decision making. A small group of parents agreed with the disgruntled parent. These posts stated that they did not want the principal to make any decisions, even if it meant leaving out opportunities for economically disadvantaged children.

Throughout the week, the blog posts got worse. They were extremely hard to read and reading them affected the principal deeply. The principal was a strong leader, but found that reading the blogs were debilitating. The posts were like standing in front of a dartboard, with each dart that was tossed piercing the skin. The inner pain and discomfort were more than the principal wanted to endure. Life outside of the principalship was terrific, and the principal refused to have work issues affect her private life.

So, the principal made a decision to stop reading those blogs!

LIGHTNING ROD GRANDMA

A grandmother came to the school's main office to complain about some bullying issues her grandson was having. The child was telling the grandmother that he was repeatedly bullied by children in his class. Upon meeting with the principal, his grandmother was told that her grandson often started some of the situations that he complained about. The grandmother was told that the school always investigated allegations of bullying, as it had zero tolerance for such behavior. The grandmother became enraged and started calling the principal names. She screamed and cursed openly in the office, using profanity toward the principal. The Grandma then said, "You think you are cute. I will floor you right here!" and then lunged at the principal to hit her with her wooden cane. The school aide jumped in to stop the assault since the principal was six months pregnant. The school aide then escorted the grandmother out of the building.The principal was granted permission to give the grandmother a limited access letter. Eventually the grandparent petitioned for the grandchild to be transferred to another school within the district. The transfer was granted.

THE AWARDS THAT BACKFIRED

There is no better way to end the year than with celebrations! In one school, the principal always made sure to organize a great luncheon for the staff. One year, the principal wanted to add what she thought would be a little humor to the day. The principal worked with a committee of teachers to create the awards. The group decided to match the awards to teachers in a fun-loving way, based on their personalities. The group also thought of situations that may have occurred throughout the year. The group also wanted to integrate some of the humorous situations that occurred during the year.

As the awards were presented at the end-of-term party, they were met with thunderous applause. Or was it really applause indicating approval or sheer disapproval of the award idea in general. At the end of the day, the principal was approached by the union representative, who informed her that the idea was insensitive and not well received by many of the teachers. The principal was shocked and quickly apologized for making people feel uncomfortable. The principal explained that the awards were meant to be humorous and not to make the staff feel uncomfortable. The principal apologized again, not only to the union representative but to the entire staff. Even though the principal apologized several times, she was still reported and investigated for misconduct.

IT WASN'T ME

It is normally understood in a school that when the principal is out of the building, the assistant principal is in charge. In this situation, that was not the case. One school day, the principal happened to be out of the building for medical reasons. During the day, there was a serious behavioral incident that occurred involving a student. School regulations require that when there is an incident of a serious nature involving a child, it must be logged into the central databank. Although the assistant principal was aware of the procedure, the information was not entered into the system.

When the principal returned to work, the principal and assistant principal met to discuss how things unfolded during the absence. Although they discussed several situations, none of which were serious, the assistant principal never informed the principal of this particular serious incident. Several weeks passed with nothing unusual occurring and no discussion about the student, when two special investigators walked into the school. They asked to speak with the principal and proceeded to ask questions about the incident. The principal told the investigators that the assistant principal was in charge that particular day since the principal was absent. The assistant principal was called to the office and recounted the specifics of the incident to the investigators. The investigator asked for a copy of the incident report, but the assistant principal was unable to adhere to that request since it had not been documented at all.

A few weeks later, the principal received an email to report for a hearing and responded to the email by saying that the assistant principal was in charge for the day and asking if the assistant principal should attend the hearing. The investigators responded that the principal should attend and not the assistant principal. They also asked the principal to bring in medical documentation for the day in question. At the hearing, the principal was questioned about the incident in depth, yet could offer limited knowledge about the specifics surrounding the incident due to being absent that day. The investigators requested that the principal send in paperwork support that the absence was for medical reasons. Although confused by their request, the principal complied. They then asked, "Can you specifically explain what this diagnosis is?" The question surprised the principal, who recognized the quandary.

Several days passed and the principal suffered numerous sleepless nights. The principal was incensed by the situation and couldn't understand being held responsible for something that happened during an absence. Given that this was not the principal's first investigation, she made the decision to resign.

THE VACATIONING TEACHER

In inner-city junior high schools, there is usually extra, out-of-classroom staff to meet the needs of the students. Some of these positions include summer school responsibilities. During one principal's first year, one such teacher, Ms. Palmer, came into the office to announce that her arrangement with the former principal included that she "never worked" in the summer, even though it was part of the job description. She was a "senior teacher," she said, and then handed the principal a paper for the superintendent that she said must be signed. The principal responded that they would consult with the superintendent and let Ms. Palmer know of their decision.

The principal never signed the paper and Ms. Palmer never showed up for the critical first day of summer school. When called at home to inquire why she was not there, she responded, "I told you, I do not work summer school!" The principal then informed her that the permission was not granted and if she did not show up, he would be forced to reassign her. She never showed up for summer school.

Before the beginning of the school year, Ms. Palmer appeared in the office with her United Federation of Teachers representative. She explained that she was unhappy with her new assignment and thought she had seniority for her out-of-classroom position. She also informed the principal that her fifty-year old son was getting married and she would be absent for the whole month of November. Her union representative pleaded her case based on her seniority. The principal said they would get back to them. After consulting with her mentor and fellow principals, the principal had a meeting with Ms. Palmer and the union representative. The principal explained what a long-term leave of absence entailed and added that this might be a solution that would please everyone. Ms. Palmer agreed and applied immediately. The principal was able to hire a wonderful teacher who was happy to work summer school. Ms. Palmer had her extended summer vacation and was available to plan her once-in-a-lifetime trip to Europe.

ASSEMBLY NIGHTMARE

SCHOOL AUDITORIUM

WELCOME

Every year, schools in many states celebrate the profession of school principals. Principal for a Day has traditionally been a great way to highlight the work of school leaders. An eager new elementary school principal decided to partner with a local community organization to participate in the event. The organization's responsibility was to screen and suggest people who were interested in spending a day with the principal.

As expected, the organization suggested a particular celebrity to spend the day with the principal. An added bonus to the visit was an assembly for the children that would be nothing short of spectacular. The principal was excited at the prospect of not only having a celebrity spend the day with her, but also an assembly filled with music and dancing for her students.

As the classes walked into the auditorium, the room was filled with the sound of instruments from the band preparing to play. There was a buzz of delight from the children, staff, and school administrators. After ten minutes, the stage was set, the lights were dimmed, and the performers were announced. As the music started, several dancers graced the stage.

Suddenly, things took a completely unexpected turn. The dancers began twerking, gyrating, and shaking their bodies across the stage. The dancing was vulgar and extremely inappropriate for the children. The principal sat in disbelief, shock, and embarrassment. How could she have allowed such an event to take place in her school? She trusted the organizers and the celebrity, and was ashamed to see such an appalling event in her school. While she noticed that most of the teachers sat expressionless, she observed the confused and disappointed faces of the parents. She was also mesmerized by the giggles, cheers, and loud laughter from the children. The event ended after thirty minutes of dancing filled with sexual innuendo not appropriate for elementary school children.

The principal left the auditorium and immediately went to her office to discuss the event with the celebrity. Although she didn't want to insult them, she made it clear that they should have been more sensitive to young children. She let them know that the event did not represent the respectful environment her students and community expected at her school. She also reached out to the community partner and informed them about the incident. Due to the nature of the event, she decided to never partner with the celebrity again. She also made sure to preview all future assemblies.

HINDSIGHT IS TWENTY-TWENTY VISION

During the ninth year as a principal, a father who was a traveling salesman had been away for several months. He came to the main office, asking to surprise his daughter. It was winter, and he was wearing a winter sports jacket, unzipped, which was not unusual as the building was heated.

I notified the teacher that the father was on his way to the classroom. The teacher and her assistant were busy getting the four-year-old children in their classroom ready for dismissal. Because it was winter, there were lots of jackets, scarves, and mittens to put on. The teachers were distracted as they were busy getting the children ready for dismissal.

The principal's door was open as the father walked his child to the front door, so he peeked in and said, "Thank you." The principal noticed his jacket was now zipped and bulged, but thought nothing of it. Dismissal took place and the teachers returned to their room. Within minutes, the principal received a call that their purses were missing. Apparently, the father's jacket was closed for a reason. The teachers were too busy to lock the door to the closet where they kept their purses. The police were called and traced the father to his apartment. Along the way, they found some of the purses' contents strewn on the ground. He was arrested and taken to the precinct, but charges were not pressed since all was recovered.

NEW CLASS TEACHER WOES

A parent who had been a member of the school for three years called the principal in the early part of August. She was very upset because she wanted to know who her child's teacher would be in September. She stated that she had attended several parties with other parents who had received welcome letters from their new teachers. She was angry that there was no clarity about who would be teaching her child's class and wanted to know why there was no certainty for teacher selection. She insulted the principal by questioning her competence and qualifications for the position. She stated that the principal should always know in June who the teacher would be for the next year. She said that her child was extremely stressed by the situation, as all of her peers were excited about knowing who their teacher would be.

The principal informed the parent that often teachers decide to take new positions over the summer and there are times when teachers simply take leaves of absence for various reasons including maternity, sabbatical, restoration of health, or personal matters. The principal explained that because of this, it is often difficult to say with certainty who will be teaching each particular class. The principal also explained that a welcome letter to families was not mandatory, but rather a courtesy meant to begin the process of building relationships between families and teachers. Although the school encouraged teachers to send out welcome letters, some teachers opted not to while others preferred a welcome phone call days before the beginning of school. This was generally the case for teachers hired in late August.

The parent was assured that if she did not receive a letter, the school would have many people to help her child locate her new teacher on the first day of school.

SECTION SEVEN:

Professional Situations, All Things Said and Done!

INTRODUCTION

As the leader of the school, a principal has to make decisions, and, even when things become unsettling, they must hold their composure. Given the many different situations and personalities a principal has to learn to maneuver, it's no wonder that they learn to become masters at identifying and responding appropriately. Not only is it important for them to know the personalities, but also how to convey information to those who may be unpredictable at best. Despres (2004) maintains that educational leadership is a complexity of practices that calls for systematic thinking. School administrators must deal with a multitude of people and events, and it is the assessment of and the response to these events that is essential to the decisions and subsequent consequences. Additionally Despres (2004) postulates "systemic thinking and its application in education leadership draws from this research in business-education partnerships and it provides an organizing means of understanding the interconnectedness of life events." (p 1)

He emphasized that linear problem solving in dealing with life events is not sufficient, because it is not about one episodic experience. These events include factors associated with that particular encounter which may shed light on the leader's responses and solutions (pp. 2–3).

The notion of deciphering personalities can present on-going challenges to both senior and new principals. How does a school administrator learn the skill of buffering potentially explosive situations with staff? They learn to think quickly and define positional stances with their staff. This is especially critical since they are directly charged with supervising and disciplining them accordingly. However, the idea of learning to relate to personalities moves beyond the school level to district administrators as well. Many school leaders tend to limit their thoughts about their concerns, discussions, and intermingling with their supervisors. Yet, there are those who speak in principal circles to one another about their relationships with district personnel, including instructional support staff, deputy superintendents, and superintendents. In these circles of confidential discussions, there is safety amongst peers. This is also a place where support and information about how to interact with supervisors can be priceless. It is of the utmost importance that a new principal partner with another principal, preferably a seasoned one, to learn how to untangle the web of the vast and multidimensional personalities they will encounter in and outside of the school building.

As far as school staff is concerned, the exchanges that take place between a teacher and a school administrator can spread in a school like wildfire, often in a matter of only minutes. One disciplinary conference that ends in a letter to file will circulate in the school, causing stress for the entire pedagogical body. This, often self-set fire, filters down to the school administrator, creating trust issues that are often difficult for the principal to resolve. The manner in which one perceives the relationship with a supervisor is monumental to the notion of trust.

TONE IS EVERYTHING

A district-level representative wanted a newly appointed principal to implement a program that many of the schools in the district were also participating in. The program was not mandated, and two of the teachers in the school did not wish to participate in the launch. Once the professional development was scheduled, the two teachers who did not want to participate went into the room for the professional development seminar. The day was a mandated professional development day, and they had not been given an alternate assignment for the day. The district representative saw the two teachers walk into the room and began yelling at the principal, saying "What are they doing here? I don't want them here!" She continued to scream at the principal. The principal responded, "Where are they supposed to go, it's a professional development day?" The district representative continued screaming at the principal, and the principal responded with, "Wait, who do you think you are talking to? Don't talk to me like that!" Tension heightened and the two walked to opposite sides of the room.

Following this incident, the relationship between the principal and the district representative became quite contentious. The principal wanted to develop a school community grounded in trust. She believed that the district representative no longer supported her. In the upcoming weeks, the representative reported several incidents of misconduct by the principal. The principal stated that the reports were unfair and mostly retaliatory because of their strained relationship. Following the investigations, which were substantiated, the principal was removed from her school and ultimately resigned her position.

FINGER SNAP ATTACK

When it becomes necessary to meet with a teacher for conduct purposes, things can become quite interesting. During a disciplinary conference, a teacher began yelling at a principal because she was not pleased with the nature of the discussion. As the meeting continued, the teacher became louder and was visibly upset with the principal.

As the meeting concluded, and they were leaving the room, the teacher turned around and snapped her fingers in the principal's face several times, grazing his nose with her fingers. The principal was shocked and told the teacher that she just hit him in the nose. She said, "You were snapping at me, so I'm snapping at you." The principal let her know that he never snapped at her at all. Then she clapped her hands in the direction of the principal. The teacher insisted that she heard finger snapping and assumed it was coming from the principal.

The principal made sure that the meeting was documented in the form of a disciplinary letter to the teacher's file.

PREPPING FOR BREAKFAST?

Early in September, the children are generally working on becoming acclimated to their new classroom environments. Teachers are getting to know the children, building community, and setting class rules and expectations with their students. During the second week of school, while conducting a walkthrough of classes, a principal opened the door to a first grade classroom during the second period of the day. Sitting in the back of the room were four teachers who were on a professional period. Gathered nearby were twenty five children working in coloring books as they waited for their class to begin.

As the principal stood in front of the room, his eyes widened with a look of disbelief. The teachers quickly gathered up all of their belongings and, one by one, they scurried past the principal, apologizing and dispersing to their classrooms, each one quickly passing the principal who remained at the classroom door. That day, the principal visited each of those teachers individually to express his dissatisfaction. The principal let them know that he expected their behavior to change. And just in case word of the incident did not make its way to everyone by word of mouth, the principal shared his expectations for appropriate behavior at the next staff conference. From that day forward, no similar incident occurred.

I BELONG IN KINDERGARTEN!

Working as a team across a grade can be one of the most rewarding learning experiences for a classroom teacher. In one school, five teachers had been working together in kindergarten, for more than six years. Between them, they had more than fifty years of experience working with children. During their final year working together, the teachers became entangled in several arguments, some of which filtered out of their classrooms and into the hallway. Both parents and other staff members witnessed their spats. In April, as the teachers prepared for reorganization, three of the teachers met with the principal to share that the group was experiencing difficulty working together. They were having altercations that were verbally insensitive to one another and there was a sense of unrest amongst the team. The principal was very aware of the rumblings, and informed the teachers that she would be meeting with all of them to discuss their preferences for the next school year.

Upon posting the new assignments in early June, the teachers noticed that a few of them would be moving up to first grade. Two weeks after the posting, one of the teachers asked to speak with the principal. The teacher shared that she believed she was the best teacher in kindergarten. She implored the principal to leave her in that grade, as she believed she was truly the finest and brightest teacher available for kindergarten. The teacher left the discussion with the principal with the final words, "I belong on this grade level. It's what I'm supposed to do and where I'm supposed to be. I don't see myself working on any other grade." The principal replied, "How can that be when your license states you can teach from first through sixth grade?"

The principal, in collaboration with the assistant principal, decided not to change the preference sheet since it was not only in the best interest of the children but also best for the entire team. Both administrators had witnessed several altercations between the two teachers throughout the year, and it was clear that a change was necessary. The teacher in question, as noted by her colleagues, was one of the most difficult personalities on the grade, creating a sense of unrest and dissension among all the teachers. She ultimately decided to transfer to a different school on the grade level she really wanted.

THE GARBAGE CAN

A first-year principal walked into a classroom on their first day on the job and noticed that children were assigned seats in groups. One student was sitting at a desk, in a closet, facing the garbage cans and a door. When asked, "Why are you sitting here?" He responded by shouting, "Because I hate myself." The principal said, "No, baby, you don't hate yourself, go to your seat." He said, "This is my seat, this is where my teacher put me." The principal said, "No, that's not your seat, this seat is by the garbage can and you are too handsome to sit near a garbage can." Then the principal introduced herself, but didn't tell him that she was the principal. The principal put his desk in the center of the classroom, facing the blackboard. The teacher turned around and said, "What are you doing?

Get out of my room! Don't move anything in my room." The principal said, "You don't have a room. Just like he doesn't have a seat, you don't have a room! We do not have children sit near garbage cans." She said, "You don't know him and you don't know his brother. He and his family belong by the garbage can. You don't know them." The principal said, "Do not move his desk!"

The principal did a few things to make some changes right away. First, all of the individual desks in the room were immediately replaced with tables, which gave the children opportunities to work in groups as opposed to sitting and working alone. The teacher was written up for her interaction with the principal and her unprofessional attitude and behavior towards the child. In order to promote a healthy environment for the child, she eventually changed classrooms. The teacher left the school.

PARENT BLINDSIDED

A first-grade teacher told the principal that one of her students did not know simple number facts. The teacher noted this on the child's report card and did not receive any response from the parents. The teacher called the mother and asked to meet with her. Rather than meeting with the teacher, the mother went directly to the principal. The mother explained that this was the fault of the teacher and that she could not believe this about her son. She said, "My husband had a doctorate from MIT in mathematics and you are telling me that my son does not know his simple math number facts." The principal immediately responded, straight-faced, "Perhaps your husband could help your son learn his number facts." The mother quickly got up from her chair and left the principal's office.

SECTION EIGHT:

Student Pick-up and Drop off

INTRODUCTION

Working as an administrator calls for long work hours in the school. Many principals begin their days as early as six thirty in the morning and work extremely long hours into the evening.For example, a principal can work between twelve and fifteen hours a day. The night owls stay until the custodian closes the building. For many principals, especially those new to the position, finding a balance between home and work can be exceptionally difficult. Working alongside a seasoned principal can be helpful, as an experienced principal understands that the work is never-ending. There is always more to do.

Working parents may leave their children outside of a school building as early as six thirty in the morning. This occurs throughout the school year, even in frigid temperatures. When the principal and other school staff arrive, they can encounter multiple children waiting to enter the school. However, the schools do not open to children until breakfast is served. Some principals have worked with their PTAs to organize support for working parents. These programs come at a cost to families, and teachers come in early to monitor children who need an early arrival. But what happens to children who cannot afford to pay the fee to come in from the cold? How does the school balance the influx of early arrivals when adequate staff many not be available to accommodate the number of students? This child-care issue is a sensitive challenge for many principals.

At the same time, teachers, principals, and safety agents are all human. When it's freezing outside, what do you do when you see a little one huddled up in a corner waiting to enter the comfort of a warm hallway? It's an on-going issue that is difficult to resolve, however many school leaders have creatively designed equitable solutions.

On the flip side, dismissal time can be quite hectic for everyone. Teachers must have superior wits about them and know the people responsible for picking up children. Even with good procedures in place, students can sometimes get lost during the process. For this reason, a principal must enlist the entire staff to support children as they prepare to head home. There are also the children who are left until the late afternoon. When school is over, children go home in many different ways. They travel by bus, are picked up by a caregiver, or, with permission, many walk home from their neighborhood schools.

What many people don't know is that some children are left in the school for hours following the dismissal of the regular day. Staff members use emergency cards to call late parents anticipating that someone will pick up the phone. The issue here is that some phones have been disconnected or the call goes straight to voicemail. Parents who work may have made arrangements for someone to pick up their child, but sometimes those arrangements go awry if the escort encounters an emergency. Therefore, staff could be waiting until late in the evening.

Sometimes the parents are gracious and thankful for the wait. However, there are those times when they don't understand that waiting takes an emotional toll on the child. The staff, many of whom have children, are forced to make arrangements for their own children. Keep in mind that this wait is not a part of the job. It simply becomes the human aspect of the work, as few principals want to call the police or even Children's Services. This is when principals demonstrate how they protect and serve the students.

CHILD CARE AT SEVEN IN THE MORNING

Teachers generally arrive at seven in the morning to talk to one another and prepare their classrooms for their students. If there is no early morning program established in the school, children are not allowed into the building until at least seven thirty, when breakfast begins. School staff at one school was beginning to notice that children were being left alone in front of the school as early as six forty-five a.m. Parents were leaving children in the rain, snow, and frigid winter temperatures, all in an effort to get to work on time. Teachers began to feel obligated to bring the children into the school. Yet no one, including school safety, wanted to be responsible for the children until the school day started at eight thirty a.m. It was a problem, since many of the teachers had already accepted children from their parents at seven.

This became a larger issue, as more parents believed they could bring children at this early morning hour.

As a community, it was understood that some parents needed early-morning childcare. Administration met and asked teachers if they wanted to come in at six forty-five to support an early-morning program. The school was able to hire two teachers to work from seven until the start of the school day. The PTA supported the early-morning program, charging early parents a fee to drop off children at seven.

A BIG SHOPPING EVENT!

The first day of school is an exciting time for most children and their families. Max was a second grader who, like most children his age, required an escort home from school. The school day ended at two-thirty in the afternoon with every child in lower school being escorted home by an adult, so it was a bit unusual to see a late child waiting for a family member in the main office. An hour ticked by and Max was still sitting. Given constant reassurance by each member of the staff punching out, the worried look still sat firmly on his face.

At four-thirty, the staff had already used Max's emergency cards, trying to contact someone to pick him up. The only number that worked was his mother's mobile number. However, after three hours of trying to reach her, the phone continued to go to voicemail. The school finally decided to order sandwiches from a local deli so that Max could have something to eat because he was hungry. At seven in the evening, the school doorbell rang. There, standing at the door with several large shopping bags, was his mom. As she floundered, pulling her large, overstuffed bags through the front doors, she said, "I came to get my son. I was shopping because my favorite store had a big sale and I couldn't miss it."

As she walked in to sign him out, she continued to share the details of the sale. She signed Max out, told him to take some of her bags, and left. She didn't ask Max how his first day went or apologize to him for being late. She left the school without thanking the staff who had stayed with Max and made sure he was safe.

The principal called Max's house early the next morning to speak with Max's mother. She informed Max's mom that the school did not uproot children out of the school to local precincts. She also took the opportunity to let his mother know how nervous Max was as he waited for someone to pick him up. She spoke with her about the importance of prioritizing her time and ensuring the safe and timely pick up of her son. Max's mother insisted that she could not miss the one day sale.

The principal explained that shopping was an unacceptable reason for being late. She also told Max's mother that being late also preyed on the emotions and sense of security of her child. Finally, the principal let her know that she would be given a one-time grace period. She added that if another similar incident occurred in the future, she would be forced to notify children's services, as her actions were a form of neglect. At that point, Max's mother became silent and then began to apologize profusely. She said that she was wrong and swore that it would never happen again. Max remained in the school through fifth grade, and his mother or a family member was always on time to pick him up.

THANKSGIVING PIES

As the school quickly emptied out at three o'clock the afternoon before Thanksgiving, Sara, a first grader, sat in the main office in a chair next to a trusted school aide. After thirty minutes and several attempts to reach out to the family, the school aide informed the administrators that no family could be reached. She gave them the emergency cards and left to see her family for the holiday. With the building completely silent, the two administrators continued to make calls to the home, both laughing at their own tardiness for waiting so long to find turkeys for their own dinner tables. As they continued to call the child's house, they made a list of the food they still needed to purchase that evening in preparation for their families' dinners. At about six o'clock, someone finally answered the phone. It was Sara's mother. She was informed that her child was still in school. She yelled out, "Marcus, you forgot to pick up Sara from school! The school is on the phone and they said that she is still there." She returned to the phone, saying, "Oh no I didn't even know that she wasn't home. I'm sitting here making pies for tomorrow. I'm coming right now." When she arrived about twenty minutes later, she came in the office with a huff. "I'm so sorry, I was cooking my pies and prepping my food for tomorrow and I'm almost ready. I didn't even know Sara wasn't home. I thought her brother picked her up. I'm so sorry, I'll send you some pie on Monday."

The two administrators let Sara's mother know that they didn't understand how she couldn't account for her child at home. They let her know that although they understood how much cooking the holiday required, she still had a primary responsibility of ensuring the safety and welfare of her daughter. They reiterated that she should know where all of her children are directly after school. This was particularly the case since her child was a first grader. They saved the discussion about children's services and let the mother know that it was important to monitor her time more effectively in the future. Mother left very happy that her child was safe and thanked the administrators repeatedly for their time. Wishing everyone a happy holiday, they all left the building together.

DISMISSAL NIGHTMARE

Dismissal procedures can be one of the most stressful parts of a school day. School staff have collected emergency cards from families and perused them to become familiar with who can pick up a student from school. They must also be aware of sole custody issues as well as persons who are not allowed access to the child. Teachers, of course, are on high alert making sure that the children are dismissed in a safe and orderly manner. However, sometimes things do not go exactly as planned.

On a warm spring day about three in the afternoon, a teacher assembled her students for dismissal near the front of the classroom door. The procedure was for each parent or caregiver to enter the class, sign the child out, put on their coat, and take them home. On this particular day, Ernest came in to pick up his niece Zalinia. As usual, parents, aunts, and uncles fluttered about, extending their farewells. Zalinia, an unusually small kindergarten student, fidgeted near the classroom door. Although she was a rambunctious and inquisitive little one, she always waited in the same spot, in the classroom directly next to the door. Ernest arrived at approximately five after three to pick up Zalinia, and with a quick wave of the hand, he and the teacher acknowledged one another and the child left the room.

At approximately ten after three, Ernest walked back into the classroom to ask if Zalinia was there. The teacher was shocked, and said, "No she's not, she went with you. I just saw you, you waved, and she went out of the room with you." He responded, "No, I don't have her. I came back to see if she was here with you." There was no time to wait, so together they scrambled to see if the child walked into another kindergarten class, but Zalinia was nowhere to be found. At three fifteen, a woman walked in the school and announced that she found a crying child a block away from the school building. As she walked toward the safety desk, the teacher and Ernest saw the child with the stranger. The teacher thanked the woman for bringing Zalinia back to the school. Ernest appeared shaken and immediately left the building to take Zalinia home.

The next day, the parent of the child came in to see the principal and the teacher to discuss the problem with Zalinia's dismissal. The teacher explained that once the child was with her uncle, she was safe. The parent insisted that because there was no signature in the sign-out book, the child was technically still in the care of the school. After carefully working through the dismissal event, it was clear that although the procedure to sign the child out was missed, her uncle became distracted and took his eyes off the child, ultimately losing sight of her. It was suggested that the family have a conversation at home to ensure that all eyes remained on the child in the future. The principal verbally reprimanded the teacher for failing to follow the student sign-out procedure.

RUNAWAY CHILD

At the end of the school day, during dismissal, a child was in crisis on the third floor of an elementary school building. School Safety personnel walked him down to the main office to see the principal. Once the child made it to the first floor, he tried to run out of the school. A staff member called for the principal, who had a strong relationship with the student. She immediately began to talk to the child in an effort to help him relax and settle him down. A teacher walked into the main office and noticed the principal restraining the child.

At that point, the principal picked up the child and brought him into her office to prevent him from hurting himself. About thirty minutes later, the police came to the school stating that an anonymous call was made stating that a child was being assaulted. The principal assured the officer that the child was fine and that there was no assault, simply restraint. At that point, the child was still sitting on the floor in distress, while the principal continued to calm the child.

A few days later, two investigators visited the school to speak with the principal. They also interviewed the teacher who was in the main office during the situation. Following the investigation, the situation was resolved.

SECTION NINE:

Shaky Ground and Good Deeds

INTRODUCTION

Leadership plays a critical role in a school's effectiveness, improvement, vitality, and growth. The way to best ensure success is by understanding organizational culture and leadership, since "leadership is involved in the creation of culture and at every stage of the organization's growth and maturity" (Schein, 2017).

There is no one way to solve every problem, but a principal has to know how to handle every situation. Problems can range from unexpected visitors, police situations, personnel meltdowns, and, of course, unlimited emotional support to the community and staff. The way that a school leader deals with these situations must be in line with the school's culture. There is an expectation that the decisions are predicated on specific protocols that have been established and must be sustained.

The decisions the principal makes ultimately shape and mold the culture and climate of a school community. Just when a principal thinks they have experienced it all, another situation pops up. Today, a principal is expected to be a therapist, politician, and arbitrator and have solutions to any situation that arises. The important thing for a principal to remember is to handle every issue with openness and a calm demeanor.

CLOSURE

For six years in early September, a challenged elderly woman came by the school to register for first grade. She always came into the office and asked to speak with the school aide. Stopping in front of the main office counter, she would ask, "Can someone help me, I need to register for first grade." Her request was always the same, once a year for six years. One September morning, she came into the office, again requesting to register for first grade. A school aide shouted, "Get her out of here! Get her out of here now! Every year I tell you to stop coming in here, but you keep coming!" The principal, hearing the commotion, walked out of her office and asked the woman, "How can I help you, ma'am?"

As the principal walked closer to the woman, the office staff began screaming out, "Don't go near her, she's crazy, stay back!" But the principal continued, smiling as she stepped closer to the frail woman. "I was a student in this school, and I want to come back to register myself for first grade. My life is bad, but in first grade, my life was good. I want to go back to my class." The principal responded, "Oh alright, so you want to register yourself as a student in our first grade class. Well, let's take a walk to your old class. Show me where it is?" The principal escorted her to the room that she said was her first-grade classroom. They opened the door and the old woman walked in slowly and quietly. She looked around the room, gazing at the walls and the furniture, picking up small items throughout the room.

For a while, neither of them said a word to one another. Then the principal asked, "Do you think you can fit into these small chairs? Soon there will be lots of small children coming in, do you think you will feel comfortable sitting here all day?" Again, the old woman stood looking around the room, remaining very quiet. She then said, "These chairs are small and I'm so big. Yes, I'm too big. I'm glad I came here. I was able to see my room. This is where my life was happy." The principal gently placed her hand on the woman's back, and guided her out of the room toward the front doors of the school. The woman thanked her for letting her see the classroom. She walked out of the building and never returned.

The principal spoke with the office staff about their tone and demeanor when speaking with the public. She provided training on the importance of creating an environment that was fair, respectful, and equitable to all members of the community, regardless of race, age, disability, or religion.

CAMOUFLAGE

At around five in the afternoon on a school day, a teenager pulled a gun on several middle school students sitting in a park adjacent to a school building. Moments later, a former student, Calim, stopped by to visit with his former principal. More than two years had passed since Calim graduated, so the principal was very happy to see the young man. Without hesitation, the principal shook Calim's hand and graciously welcomed him into the office. Although Calim was bright, he had struggled in school both socially and in terms of making good decisions, so it was no surprise that the principal was interested in talking to him to see how things were going in his academic, social, and family life.

They sat together for more than twenty minutes, talking about how things were progressing for Calim. Suddenly, the phone rang and the school secretary informed the principal that he had visitors in the main office who wanted to speak with him. The principal hung up the phone and made plans to talk to the student at a later date. They shook hands and both agreed that the time together was well spent. Calim opened the door to walk out when four kids screamed out in unison, "That's the guy, he's the one who pulled a gun on us!" Calim was detained briefly and then handcuffed and taken into police custody. The principal was shocked when he realized that Calim used the school to hide from his situation. As a result, the principal fully cooperated with the police, documented the incident, and reported it to the district superintendent.

UNHINGED AND RATTLED

In early October, an assistant principal was placed in a school to provide support to a senior principal. Together they discussed how the assistant principal could best support the needs of the principal, teachers, and students. They decided that he had a strong understanding of curriculum and he would plan a series of professional development workshops for teachers.

As the days progressed, the assistant principal began to exhibit signs of paranoia. He was fearful of everyone around him, and believed that they had an ultimate plan to destroy him. The problem became more frightening, as he began to see things in the room that were not there. Due to the delusions he was having, the principal was concerned that his judgment and mental capacity were challenged. Subsequently, she began to fear for herself, the community, and most of all, the children. As a result of his behavior, the assistant principal was sent for a medical evaluation and was found unfit for duty.

TEACHER'S MOTHER TAKING CHARGE

One day, a principal walked into a kindergarten classroom across from her office and witnessed the teacher lying prone on the floor. The children in the classroom were playing around her, ignoring the situation. The principal asked the teacher to get up and arrange to meet with her later that day. At the meeting, the teacher explained that she was having a bad day and her nerves were on edge.

She just needed a rest. She also revealed that she was on medication for mental health issues.

The principal advised her that a meeting was required with the superintendent and she could bring her union representative. She arrived with her mother, who claimed the principal did not understand that her daughter was having issues and needed to be handled very gently. The principal explained that the main role of the principal is to provide a climate conducive for education, characterized by safety and orderliness. A teacher lying down in the middle of the classroom with her eyes closed because she could not cope, was not acceptable teacher behavior and dangerous. The teacher's mother stood up and began yelling at the principal. She explained that the principal should be thinking about her poor daughter and forget about the children for once.

The teacher was put on leave until a formal hearing determined whether or not to terminate her.

BEST-LAID PLANS

Often, principals develop relationships with grandparents in the absence of the parents. In this case, Grandma was the guardian for a third grader named Edmond. He was a very bright young man, but did not want to be in school. Edmond hid every morning simply because he did not want to go to school. When his grandma finally got him into school, he always refused to go to class. When Grandma was successful at convincing him to go to class, it would only last a short time. Within an hour of the start of the school day, he left the class to roam the halls aimlessly. As a whole, Edmond openly refused to follow any school rules, and this was only September.

The principal worked collaboratively with the assistant principal to use a variety of strategies to improve student behavior. Edmond was given rewards for appropriate behavior. At one point, he was given the role of hall monitor. He was also told that if he made it through the majority of the day without leaving his class, he could use the gym to play basketball after school. This incentive was great, because playing ball was something that Edmond really loved to do.

Grandma and the principal became very close and the principal always listened as she told stories about Edmond's struggle with missing his mother. Grandma's main goal was ultimately to keep her grandson in school, alive, and out of trouble. She depended on the principal for help, as she had no one else she could turn to. Over the next few weeks, the principal built a great relationship with Edmond, and sometimes they had lunch together and talked about many things. One day, the principal asked him to share the one thing he really wanted, which turned out to be an iPod. At the time, an iPod was an expensive, four-hundred dollar electronic device.

The principal made a deal with him that if he worked hard on his academics, stayed in class, and did not give his grandma problems at home, he would be rewarded with an iPod in June. His grandmother loved the idea, and everyone agreed to move forward with that plan in mind.

For a while, Edmond followed the behavior plan and was doing very well. He met daily with the principal to celebrate areas of success and plan on improving those areas he found challenging. While it would be nice to share that the plan had a happy ending, it turned out that the iPod wasn't what Edmond really wanted. He was missing the love of his mother who was in prison. The reality is that sometimes, principals can create the best behavior plan, in the best interest of the child, but it still may not work.

DANCING AT SCHOOL

As a result of a grant, schools had the opportunity to offer an after-school enrichment program that included ballroom dancing. The principal hired a professional dancer and the students loved the classes, which were very well attended. When parents heard about the program, they asked the principal to offer dance classes to the parents as well. The principal believed that this would be a way to bring parents into the school for a positive experience. After the second session, the parents came to see the principal complaining that the teacher was too rough and they could dance on their own. In addition, the parents disliked the instructor's musical selections and demanded the principal fire the instructor. The principal explained that the instructor had a signed contract for eight sessions and they were to attend. Surprisingly, the parents attended the whole series of lessons, saying they did not want their children to become better dancers than them.

STAGE MOTHER

The principal of a large elementary school reported that every year the music teacher produced an extravagant holiday concert. The show featured several hundred students singing onstage, as well as a group of dancers who had to audition for the show. The dancers were required to attend an important rehearsal the day before Thanksgiving break. That day was always scheduled on parent–teacher conference day, which meant the music teacher was free to work on choreography. Parents whose children were dancers had to sign a permission slip, agreeing that if their child missed the rehearsal they could not dance in the show.

On rehearsal day, all of the dancers showed up except one girl. The school called the home to make sure the parent did not forget about the rehearsal, but no one answered the phone. The music teacher removed the girl from the dance portion as she would not know the routines, but allowed her to participate in the choir portion of the show. After Thanksgiving break, the child's mother met with the music teacher to explain why she did not bring her daughter to the rehearsal. She said that the family decided to go on a cruise and they could not pass up the opportunity. However, she wanted her daughter to be taught the choreography and put back into the dance performance. The music teacher reminded her that she had been informed about the mandatory attendance at the rehearsal and that she had signed the permission slip that detailed this information. The mother became irate and stormed into the principal's office. The principal reiterated what the music teacher said and the mother became very angry, yelling and storming out of the office.

The mother, not satisfied with the principal's response, drove directly to the superintendent's office to file a complaint. The superintendent told the mother that he was leaving the decision up to the principal. Not happy, the mother contacted the local newspaper and asked to speak to a reporter. She told the reporter that the school was discriminating against her daughter because she went on a cruise. Before printing the story, the reporter checked with the principal who told the entire story. The story never appeared in the newspaper.

WHERE'S MAX?

A school custodian is one of the most important people in a school community. They are responsible for opening the school, providing heat, and keeping the school clean.

They are essential personnel who ensure the building is ready and prepared for safe operations every day. Once the building check is done in the morning, the building manager or head custodian meets with the custodial staff to discuss plans for the day. Periodically, the building manager must leave for meetings, to pick up small items to support repairs, or to run other errands like picking up paychecks.

Max was a custodial building manager in one school who always seemed to have an errand to run. His main errand was to the hardware store. He left around nine thirty in the morning and reported back after one in the afternoon. The errands started as a once-a-week venture that quickly became a daily event. Since he did not check in with the principal before he left, it was difficult to determine how long he had been out of the building. Often, when he could not be found the administrators paged or called his office every thirty minutes. This helped them keep track of how long he was gone. When his staff was asked where he was, sometimes they shook their heads indicating they did not know. Other times they said that he was at the hardware store. This became a serious issue, since the building manager is a critical person in a school community.

During a practice fire drill, Max was unavailable, leaving one custodian to monitor and secure all exits. Other times he left one custodian to clean up during the school day, after school, or at special school events. It was unrealistic to expect one custodian to service all areas of a building. Unfortunately for the school, this resulted in a less than clean environment.

The principal decided to meet with Max to discuss his concerns about leaving for long hours. This did not change his behavior, and Max continued to leave for extended periods of time.

Finally, the principal contacted the head custodial supervisor, who hurried to the school to find that Max was in fact missing in action. A procedure was put in place for Max to inform the principal of his whereabouts daily. He was also disciplined by his supervisor and his time was monitored carefully for more than a year. He was eventually terminated from his position as head custodian.

WHO IS IN CHARGE?

One day while making her rounds, the principal happened to peek in the office of the social worker. She noticed that two students had a rope and were using it to tie the social worker to the chair. The principal was horrified, and ran into the room to check on the situation and immediately asked the students to untie the social worker. After the students did so, the principal asked the social worker to come out into the hall to find out what had happened. The social worker laughed and explained that the students were having issues because they felt powerless. She believed tying her up gave them a sense of power. The principal asked the social worker to meet with her later that day when she was free to discuss this inappropriate way of handling this matter.

SECTION TEN:

Closing Thoughts

INTRODUCTION

As we sat down to record our closing thoughts, we realized that since the twenty-first century has presented principals with new challenges, we needed to include additional important information that affects school leaders and their communities. There is no denying that social media has had a great impact on education and added another layer of challenges for the principal. The accelerated pace of technological change has altered the way teachers teach and the way parents and students communicate with one another and with principals and teachers. Berman (1990) posited: As educators we must inspire young people to hold a positive version of the future—to believe that we can do better, live better, be kinder, and be fairer. Students need our help if they are to develop confidence to participate in creating a more peaceful, just, and ecologically sound world … It demands that we find ways to balance personal competence with social skills and social responsibility (p 80).

Online social networking sites provide news from celebrities and relationship information, sexting, cyberbullying, and Googling of test answers that may result in students paying more attention to their phones than the teacher. Smart phones have transformed the way we communicate, but there is no question they can be an additional challenge for teachers and administrators. In schools, students carry their phones as an instant form of communication with their peers and families.

School leaders and teachers often debate whether or not phones are a deterrent to student academic performance. Are children so immersed in their use of cell phones at home and in schools that they exclude themselves from interacting with others? Does this increase the possibility of creating opportunities for social exclusion amongst the young? How do we support young people in schools with some of the challenges of cell phone use?

However, banning cell phones in schools can come with its own set of problems. Enforcement can be difficult, therefore administrators should develop a plan to instruct students in how to use their phones responsibly rather than banning the phones, as these devices can be utilized as a great teaching tool. Given the many shifts and challenges that occur during an educator's day, it is no surprise that they must learn to teach at a superior level to meet the social demands and the inquisitive nature of their classroom students.

A national study conducted by the National Association of Secondary School Principals in 2015 that examined the attributes of effective school principals found that high student performance was directly aligned to collective leadership—the shared influence of educators and the community. Principals who "champion collective leadership are involved in efforts to improve teaching and learning in addition to their management responsibilities" (p. 64).

"The most important leadership tool is the leader's self—your self. At the foundation of this principle—and at the foundation of the whole presencing approach lies this simple assumption: every human being is not one but two. One is the person who we have become through the journey of the past. The other one is the dormant being of the future we could become through our forward journey. Who we become will depend on the choices we make and the actions we take now" (Scharmer, 2009).

ADDENDUM:
DISCUSSION QUESTIONS

1. Can you identify with any particular story? Would you resolve the situation in a similar or different manner? Please describe YOUR decision/solution.

2. Which story did you find was the most difficult to arrive at a decision/solution? Please explain why.

3. As a school leader, what steps do you follow to arrive at a decision? Do you have a particular process? If so, is it your own or is it dictated by district policy?

4. School leaders' decisions many times result in establishing policy. If that has been the case for you, please describe how you communicated the new policy to staff, students and parents.

5. As a school leader many solutions must be made in a timely manner. As a result, one may need to alter that decision. Have you experienced this in your school? What were the factors that led you to decide to alter your decision?

MEET THE AUTHORS

Dr. Yolanda Ramirez has worked in the field of education for more than twenty-five years. Her experience includes that of family worker, paraprofessional, literacy coach, and assistant principal. The latter part of her work spans more than twelve years as an elementary school principal. She specializes in customized intervention for students who are at risk. Her broader and more extensive expertise, includes creating experiential learning opportunities aligned with New York City and State Standards for all children. Infused with a cross curriculum model, she has strategically planned and provided children who are English Language Learners, economically disadvantaged and those who have special needs, experiences within and outside of New York City limits. Her special interest includes learning from and supporting school leaders who work in schools that are in transition. This also includes school communities that are shifting in culture and climate as a result of gentrification in the surrounding community.

Dr. Alice Siegel has been in the field of education for almost fifty years. She has worked as a teacher and as a building and central office administrator on both the elementary and secondary levels. She holds a doctorate in educational leadership and was an associate professor at the Graduate School of Education at The College of New Rochelle. She presently serves a consultant to schools that require literacy improvement and offers pro-fessional development to teachers and principals. Additionally, she has presented her work internationally at many conferences from Africa to Europe. She has published thirteen nonfiction books for children aged eight to twelve and co-authored arti-cles on literacy-related issues that have appeared in peer-re-viewed professional journals.

Dr. Marlene Zakierski is an associate professor and direc-tor of the Russell Sage College New York City Educational Leadership Doctoral Program where she teaches, advises, and chairs school leaders' research as they pursue and attain their doctoral degrees. Additionally, she was a National Science Foundation Grant recipient. Additionally, she served as a pro-fessor and director of Literacy and Special Education Graduate Programs at Iona College where she partnered with a neigh-boring school district to create, develop, and provide a college program to support the development of postsecondary educa-tional opportunities for neurodiverse young men and women. She has authored a number of peer-reviewed journal articles and grants and presented research at many national and inter-national conferences. She served as a teacher, principal, in var-ious central office administrative positions, and as an assistant superintendent during a career that spans more than forty-five years. She continues to spend time in PreK–12 schools as a consultant who provides professional development focused on literacy, coaching, mentoring, and assisting educators to implement thought-provoking practices that lead to gains in student achievement.

MEET THE ARTISTS

Laura Brooks is a self-taught painter and mixed media artist whose work has been featured at shows in New York City, Miami, and Boston. Laura has primarily focused on portraiture to capture a compelling and complex gaze, but her recent work explores abstracted storytelling through the playful use of color, shape, and form. Laura is also a practicing lawyer, having acted as general counsel of Paddle8, an online art auction house. She lives and works in Brooklyn. You can see more of her work at lauraannebrooks.com or follow her on Instagram @lauraannebrooks.

Diana Cullingford is a retired elementary school teacher. She has taught various elementary grades in California, New York City, and Rockland County, New York. She has always been interested in art and has used that talent to enhance learning in various subjects in her classroom.

Josue Mendez is a self-taught artist whose vision has always been to change the world. His heart and soul are poured into each piece he creates. His craft and passion drives him to help make a difference for immigrants, special needs children, and LGBTQ+. As a paraprofessional, he has the opportunity to inspire his students to find new strengths with a wide range of hidden talents. Previously, Josue has completed multiple murals throughout Staten Island in various sizes. He prides himself on being able to make even the smallest vision into a masterpiece. His specialties include acrylic paintings, calligraphy, charcoal, graffiti, graphic designs, indoor and outdoor murals, pastels, and portraits. Along with private beginner classes, Josue hosts paint parties at local businesses as well as traveling to homes for special occasions! Facebook: JM Custom Art Studio Instagram: JM_Custom_Art_Studio

REFERENCES

Berman, S. (1990). Educating for social responsibility. Association of Supervision and Curriculum Development: Alexandria, VA, (pp 75–80).

Bolman, L. G., & Deal, T. E. (2008). Reframing organizations: Artistry, choice, and leadership. San Francisco, CA: Jossey-Bass.

Bolman, L. G., & Deal, T. E. (2006). The Wizard and The Warrior—Leading with Passion and Power. San Francisco, CA: Jossey-Bass.

Bennis, W. (2009). On becoming a leader. New York, NY: Basic Books.

Bennis, W. (2007). The challenges of leadership in the modern world: Introduction to the special issue. American Psychologist, 62(1), 2–5

Fullan, M. (2014). The principal: Three keys to maximizing impact. San Francisco, CA: Jossey-Bass.

Education Digest. (2011). Best principals espouse collective leadership research finds. National Association of Secondary School Principals, 58(4). Retrieved http://

www.edtrust.org/sites/edtrust.org/sites/edtrust.org/
files/thestateofeducationforafricanamericanstudents_
EdTrust_June2014.pdffrom

The state of education for African American students.
(2014). Washington, DC: The Albert Shankar Institute.
Retrieved from http://www.edtrust.org/sites/edtrust.
org/sites/edtrust.org/files/thestateofeducationforafri-
canamericanstudents_EdTrust_June2014.pdf

Goleman, D. (2014). What Makes a Leader: Why Emotional
Intelligence Matters. More Than Sound. MA: Florence.

Maulding, W. S., Peters, G. B., Roberts, J., Leonard, E., &
Sparkman, L. (2012). Emotional intelligence and resil-
ience as predictors of leadership in school administrators. Journal of Leadership Studies, 5(4), 20-26. http://
dx.doi.org/10.1002/jls.20240

Leithwood, K., Begley, P., & Cousins, B. (1990). The nature,
causes, and consequences of principals' practices: An
agenda for future research. Journal of Educational
Administration, 28(4), 5–31.

Salovey, P., & Mayer, J. D. (1990). Emotional Intelligence.
Imagination, Cognition and Personality, 9(3), 185–211.
https://doi.org/10.2190/DUGG-P24E-52WK-6CDG

Scharmer, C. Otto (2009). Theory U: Leading from the Future as it Emerges. Berettet-Koehler Publishers, INC. CA: Oakland.

Schein, E. H. (2010). Organizational culture and leadership. San Francisco, CA: Jossey-Bass.

Wheatley, M., and Kellner-Rogers, M. (1998). The paradox and promise of community. In F. Hesselbein, M. Goldsmith, R. Beckhard and R. Schubert, The community of the future. San Francisco: Jossey-Bass, pp. 9–18.